SHATTERED

A STORY OF LIFE AND DEATH

Steven Tenaglia

© 2016 Steven Tenaglia
All rights reserved.
Cover Photo: Shattered Glass © Lars Chrsitensen

The events in this book are true. Some names have been changed to protect both the innocent and the guilty.

Printed in the United States

ISBN 978-1-68419-731-6

In loving memory of
Steven Mario Tenaglia

July 28, 1998 - November 26, 2002

*Grieving the loss of a child is a process,
it begins the day a child passes
and ends the day the parent joins him.*

—B.J. Karrer

CHAPTER 1
SMITTEN

IN THE SUMMER of 1995, when I was employed as a bread man in Baltimore, Maryland, I met Angie Gibson, the bakery manager at a supermarket on my delivery route. Our relationship began as most relationships do, with the usual flirtations.

It was hard not to notice Angie; she wasn't exactly beautiful, but with her blue eyes and blonde hair, along with an aura of sexuality and danger, she commanded attention.

Maybe it was her confidence or her charm, but it was more than that. She had charisma. It was as if she held some sort of power over me; she seemed to possess a sixth sense that zeroed in on me as I delivered bread three times a week to the store where she worked.

"Hi, Steve!" She stared right into my eyes, trying to hold my gaze. "How're you this morning?"

I barely knew this woman, and the intense eye contact was too much for me, so I looked away, busying myself with the bread inventory. "I'm all right. And how are you?"

"I'm wonderful — now that you're here."

Caught off guard by this unexpected flattery, I looked up and said, "I'm sorry, but I don't know your name."

She smiled, extending her hand. "I'm Angie, and I've been watching you."

"Watching me? Why would you do that?"

"Because you're good looking, " she said, still staring. "And I can tell you're a good guy."

I felt awkward being approached like this, but she was saying what every man wants to hear. Something told me to shut this conversation down as quickly as possible, so I blurted out, "Thank you very much, but I don't want a girlfriend right now."

"Why not?" Her smile changed to a pout.

"Because I'm thinking of moving. And besides, isn't that a wedding ring on your finger?"

She finally broke eye contact, glanced at her ring, and said, "I'm separated."

"That still means you're married, doesn't it?"

"Well, I'm *working* on being separated." She stuffed her hand in her pocket. "My husband beats me."

Even though this was too much information too soon, the thought that she was being abused concerned me. "Are you okay?"

"Yeah, I'm fine... for now. But I need to move. I need to find a safe place for my two little girls. I need to get out." She paused. "I'm afraid he's going to kill me."

That was our first conversation.

From that day forward, whenever I'd deliver bread to her store, we'd find a few minutes to chat. What man wouldn't willingly spend a few minutes talking to an attractive blonde with blue eyes and a nice build? Angie was about 5' 4'' and very physical, always finding an excuse to touch my arm or my hand as I shelved bread in her store. Our conversations often centered on her husband Frank and their horrible marriage. I urged her to get some counseling, and told her to report any abuse to the police. Sometimes the conversation switched gears and she'd ask me about my life.

"Where are you planning to move anyway?" she asked one day.

"I'm going to North Carolina and grow me a ten-pound baby boy," I said, only half joking. Truth be told, I wanted a home and family more than anything in the world. I was raised Catholic by two loving parents on Long Island, the oldest of three, and I'd always wanted a family of my own. I'd left New York in 1988, nursing a broken heart and hoping to find my "happily ever after" in Baltimore. My parents had moved from Long Island a few years earlier, settling in North Carolina in 1986, after my father suffered a massive stroke. My sister moved with my parents and my brother eventually moved south as well, leaving me as the only family member not enjoying the sunny south.

My family urged me to join them. They thought a fresh start would be a good thing; they knew I was still suffering from the loss of my first love, and honestly my living conditions in Baltimore were less than ideal.

That year I listed my house in Baltimore with a realtor and made plans to join my family 400 miles to the south.

When she learned my house was on the market Angie asked, "Maybe my daughters and I could rent part of your house until it sells?" She made a strong case for their safety. "This would get us away from Frank and give me some time to look for a place of my own."

There were red flags everywhere. I told her that I didn't think it would work out for her to live there with me.

"But I'll take care of your house, keep it looking great for the realtor."

"No, I'm sorry," I said. "I just don't think it's the best idea."

A week or so later, I was stunned to see the bread I'd delivered the day before to Angie's store had been destroyed — crushed loaves, shredded wrappers had been strewn over the shelves and floor. As I assessed the damage, I heard gum popping behind me. I turned around, and there stood Angie.

"What happened?" I asked.

She told me that the assistant store manager, Robert Jones, had done it. "He saw me talking to you yesterday and it really pissed him off." She cracked her gum again. "He's got a crush on me."

All I could think to say was, "Doesn't he know that you're married?"

"He knows," she said. "He's married, too." She chomped some more on her gum, waiting for my reaction.

"Why would he ruin the bread?"

She shrugged. "He's crazy. I guess he thinks you're competition." Then she stepped closer to me and whispered, "You *are* competition, you know. I really like you."

I looked away and shifted my attention to cleaning up the mess. I saw no point in getting involved with someone just before moving to another state.

Angie touched my shoulder. "Let me show you something else." She rolled up her sleeve, exposing a new set of bruises. "Steve," she said, "I'm worried. My little girls. and I aren't safe." She pushed her sleeve down, covering the bruises. "I'm really trying to get out of there, but I can't do it on my own." She sounded desperate. "And look at this…" She pulled a folded piece of paper from the back pocket of her jeans. "It's a restraining order against Frank."

I saw the municipal court letterhead along the top of the paper and I reached for it to take a closer look, but she pulled it away and put it back in her pocket.

Even though she had "NO!" written all over her, I felt compassion for this woman who was being beaten by her husband, and for the little girls whose lives would be ruined living in a situation like she'd described.

The next thing I knew I was offering her two of the three bedrooms in my house — rent free — until it sold. In return, she would take care of the place, doing the cleaning and errands until she saved enough money to find another place.

Angie and her girls (Mary was about six years old, and Jodi was only two) moved in to my house, a cute little ranch with three bedrooms, one bath and a full basement. It sat on a corner lot with a wooden stockade fence around the back yard.

Mary seemed like her daddy's little girl. She was confused and obviously missed her father. Consequently, she acted a little rebellious toward her mother. Jodi, however, was nothing but a sweet little girl.

I viewed myself as a benevolent babysitter. They were little girls and I was a grown man. I didn't want any problems or misunderstandings, and I kept my distance.

This roommate-style living arrangement with Angie and her girls lasted for about ten months. During that time I saw how beautiful life could be with children, and it rekindled my desire to have a family of my own.

Because we were now living together, we began to be more involved in each other's day to day lives. In a previous job, I'd experienced an acid burn which had left a white blotch on my arm. I had decided to cover the scar with a Superman logo tattoo, and when I went to the tattoo parlor, Angie tagged along. While we were there, she decided to get one, too. "What should I get?" she asked me.

"I don't know," I said. "A tattoo should be meaningful. What do you like?"

"I love everything about *you*," she said.

"Well, I like roses."

She ended up with a three-inch long rose on one shoulder. It was a pretty little thing, but she'd also had my name tattooed along with the rose. That was a surprise. I was flattered, but quite honestly I thought the writing made it look a little cheap and comic-book like.

—·—

More red flags popped up, but I was able to ignore them, even when a sweet, older woman named Wilma, who worked at the same store as Angie cornered me one day when I delivered their bread. She had always treated me like a son, and I considered her a good friend. A few weeks after the bread incident, she said, "Steve, I really need to talk to you."

"Sure, Wilma. What's up?"

"Are you seeing Angie?"

Her question surprised me. "Sort of. Not really. Why?"

"Steve, please stay away from that girl. You know I love you like my own son, and I don't want you to get hurt. Stay away from her. She's dangerous."

I was so shocked to hear this that it never occurred to me to ask for details.

I thought perhaps there was some sort of power struggle going on between Wilma and Angie.

When I got home from work that night, Angie and I exchanged hugs as usual, and I said, "Wilma said something strange to me today. She warned me to stay away from you. Any idea why she'd say something like that?"

Angie's eyes flickered as she said, "That old bitch? She doesn't like me. Probably because I work harder than she does and it makes her look bad." She put her arm around my shoulders. "Maybe she's just jealous."

I never saw Wilma again. She'd been close to retirement, so when she wasn't at the store the next time I delivered bread, I assumed she had retired. Wilma's disappearance wasn't the only change at that store. Robert Jones, the man who had destroyed the bread, demoted Angie from bakery manager to stock person, and had her transferred to a different store. He didn't just have a crush on Angie; he was her former lover. Even after Angie had been transferred, he continued to vandalize my deliveries. He wasn't just jealous, he was nuts.

CHAPTER 2
FAMILY MATTERS

ALTHOUGH ANGIE and I were not in a romantic relationship, I found myself slowly being caught up in the drama of her life. Knowing our living arrangement would soon end and we'd be going our separate ways, I tried to remain detached from her family life.

However, her mother Edith was dying of cancer and one day Angie asked me to go with her to the hospital to visit. We found Edith sitting up in bed. It was apparent that she had been pretty at one time, but after the removal of a breast, an arm and a leg, she looked pale and pitiful. A powerful feeling of nothingness was present in the room. It was as if her life force had already departed and she was only partially present in that broken body, with her soul already halfway gone.

I introduced myself and said, "God bless you, Mom."

The dying woman tried to smile.

"Hi, Mom." Angie said. "How are you feeling?"

Edith whispered, "I'm all right."

About five minutes after we'd arrived, Angie's sister Dorothy joined us. She walked to the side of the bed and kissed her mother on the cheek. While kissing Edith, Dorothy peeled off the pain medication patch taped to Edith's cheek and swiftly replaced it with an obviously used one. Barely thirty seconds later, Dorothy turned and walked out of the room.

"What just happened?" I asked Angie, unable to make sense of what I'd just seen.

"What do you mean?"

"Didn't you see your sister remove your mom's pain patch and replace it with a different one? What the hell's going on?"

She looked away and said, "Stay out of it, Steve. Let it go."

I could not let it go. "Your mom is being eaten alive by cancer, and they're cutting her to pieces in order to save her. The pain must be unbearable. How could you let anyone take her pain medicine? I can't believe your sister could do something like this to her own mother!"

"Stay out of it, Steve."

Obviously Angie knew something I didn't. This was *her* family, and we weren't married — we weren't even dating — so it was really none of my business. Still, I tried to reason with Angie, but she ignored me, and after about fifteen minutes, Edith started moaning and crying, in a "begging for mercy" kind of way.

I looked at Angie and asked, "What are you going to do?"

"Let's go," she said and got up to leave.

I was amazed that she could just walk out of that room. I can't believe that I followed Angie out of the room and left that old woman moaning in pain. I was ashamed of myself. In the hall, I said, "We can't leave your mom like that. We've got to tell a doctor or a nurse."

Angie kept walking and said, "She'll be okay. This is a hospital. They'll take care of her."

I kept pleading with her, but she was walking too fast to pay attention. Because we'd arrived in separate cars, we said goodbye in the parking lot, and during my ride home I was haunted by what had happened. I felt guilty for not helping Edith, and asked myself why I hadn't been more forceful. *How could I make this right?*

The next day I asked Angie if I could go with her to the hospital again, and she agreed, thanking me for being supportive during such a sad time. I don't know what, if anything, I could accomplish by going back to the hospital, but I knew I needed to go.

This time Angie's brother Mike was there, and to my astonishment, I saw him do the same thing his sister Dorothy had done the day before. He took the pain patch and replaced it with a used one.

But this time, I did something about it. "Put that patch back on your mother right now." I said to Mike.

Angie stood and said, "Stay out of this, Steve."

Mike smirked and left the room.

"I know what I just saw," I said to Angie. "What kind of family is this?"

She said, with no emotion whatsoever, "Leave it alone, Steve. It's none of your business."

I went to the nurses' desk and soon two nurses rushed to Edith's room and found an old patch where the new one had been. The nurses switched their patient to IV meds to avoid another incident.

I had heard about drug addicts doing this sort of thing, but never imagined it would happen right in front of my eyes. Over time, as I began to piece together fragments of stories from Angie's childhood, I came to understand that Angie and her siblings had not experienced normal childhoods. I asked plenty of questions, but Angie was reluctant to discuss the past, and it didn't take long for me to stop asking.

Edith died a few days later and her funeral was small and quiet. Dorothy and Mike glared at me, still angry that I'd put a halt to their little game of swiping their mother's morphine patches.

I met another sister who Angie told me was "crazy." She weighed about 300 pounds and was one of the meanest people I'd ever encountered. She had a boyfriend, a very nice guy (and about half her size), and while Angie and I were visiting with them, the sister punched her boyfriend in the face so hard that he fell down the stairs. She punched him because he'd put a beer on the table and left a water ring.

Neither Angie's dad or older brother Jack were there. Her father had remarried, and Jack lived too far away to attend. Surprisingly, everyone else in the family described Jack as "the crazy one." I later heard that Edith had once chained him in the attic to punish him for some minor offense. It was summer and the temperature was well over 100 degrees. The story was that he'd been kept there for days, and had become so panicked that he had gnawed at his arm in order to escape. When I met him, years later, Jack seemed like the nicest member of Angie's family. I noticed that he moved his arm like a stroke victim and his forearm seemed to lack any significant muscles. Though he did have very good mobility and dexterity, he did appear handicapped by the conscious effort it took to move his arm.

At Edith's funeral, out of the blue, Angie turned to me and asked, "Can the girls and I move to North Carolina with you?"

Every bit of instinct I possessed screamed NO.

"I can't bear to let you go," she said. "I'm in love with you."

Wow. What could I say to that?

"You know, you would make a good father, Steve," she said. "I could give you that ten-pound baby boy."

I'd always wanted a son.

Our roommate status ended and Angie became my girlfriend. The next four weeks were amazing. Every day just seemed to be better than the last, and I was happy beyond words to find myself with a loving partner and two beautiful daughters. It was a dream come true, and eventually the stories of Frank and the beatings dwindled, replaced with Angie's total devotion and attention to me and to our home. Accompanied by a sweet smile, she was always saying, "I love ya!"

I felt terrible because I could not say it back.

I was not in love with her. In my deepest heart, no matter how hard I searched for that feeling, I could not find it. But I was enjoying the attention and the sense of family so much that I ignored that little fact.

My day, as a bread man, began at one o'clock in the morning. First thing, I'd head to the refrigerator and make some sort of breakfast, and I wouldn't eat again until I got home in the early afternoon.

Now, with Angie and I living together as an official couple, when I arrived home after my early morning shift, I'd find the house spotless, and lunch waiting for me in the kitchen. She was at work by that time of day, but she always left a note that read, "Sorry I missed you. Hope you like your lunch. I miss you and I love you." Sometimes she'd make me a sandwich or bring me a Big Mac and tuck a little one shot bottle of vodka in with it. Though I was not much of a drinker, I appreciated the gesture.

Sometimes, when she was out shopping for her girls, she'd pick up a shirt or pair of pants for me. It was nice to be pampered like this.

In return, I would nap after my lunch and then get up to start dinner and help Angie when she came home with her daughters around 3:30.

My house finally sold and with escrow due to close in ten days, I started packing tools, clothes and other things from the garage and basement.

One morning, at one a.m., on my way to the kitchen, I noticed the light was on in Jodi's room. I didn't hear anything so I figured everything was okay.

While I enjoyed my breakfast, I heard a noise that sounded like someone gagging. Within seconds I heard it again, but this time it sounded worse. I ran to Jodi's room and found Angie sitting at the head of the bed on the pillows, and Jodi lying at her feet. It appeared that Jodi was choking. Her face was white, her eyes were bulging, and her lips were blue. Her mouth was open, and she was gasping for air. I realized in an instant that I was totally ignorant about what to do in a situation like this, and in the next instant I realized that Angie was just sitting there. I grabbed Jodi and shoved my fingers down her throat, finding a penny lodged there. I removed the coin and lifted Jodi and slapped her back until she started breathing again. I held her tight for a few minutes while she sobbed in terror.

Angie didn't move or say a word during the whole ordeal. She made no attempt to help, nor did she show any fear or concern. She didn't express relief either that her daughter was going to be okay. I assumed she must have been in shock.

I, on the other hand, was hysterical. "How did she get a penny down her throat?"

Angie shrugged. "That's what kids do. They stick things in their mouths."

"But Angie, it's one o'clock in the morning! She was *sleeping*! How does a sleeping kid put a penny in her mouth? How could you just sit there doing nothing? Why didn't you call for me? Or call 911?"

"I don't know," she said.

I paced back and forth, completely freaked out. "You don't know? That's your child! She could have died!"

I had to go to work, though I hated to leave. I began to wonder about Angie's capabilities as a parent. "Try to get some sleep, kiddo," I said to Jodi. To Angie I said, "Maybe you should check the room for anything else that she might choke on."

After that, Jodi and I developed a special kind of bond. It seemed as though she looked up to me as her hero and stuck to me like velcro. I was honored to have the admiration of such a beautiful child, but along with that admiration came a new level of responsibility. I found that I loved being a father figure.

One day I called Angie's cell from work and there was no answer. I called several more times throughout the day, and still nothing. I was frantic with worry, and then my phone rang and it was Angie, cheerfully telling me that she was about a mile from home and would be back in a few minutes.

Before I could ask where she'd been, she hung up. When I got home, Angie and Jodi were there, but Mary was not. I asked about Mary.

"I took her to Frank's."

"Already? But we're not leaving yet." Jodi was moving with us to North Carolina, but per Angie and Frank's divorce agreement, her older daughter Mary was to remain in Baltimore with her father.

"She smells."

"What?"

"She smells like Frank, so Frank can have her a little early."

"Angie, you know, I'm a little worried about her staying with Frank. Are you sure she'll be safe?"

"Frank is a jerk, but he won't hurt her."

"How do you know that, after what he did to you?"

Then she said something that stopped me in my tracks.

"Frank never beat me."

This contradicted everything she'd told me.

"What do you mean? What about the bruises you showed me? The whole reason you wanted to move in with me was to get away from his violence. What are you telling me?"

"Leave it alone, Steve. It's none of your business."

She walked into the bedroom and closed the door, but I followed her.

"How can this be none of my business? This is my life, too. What's going on?"

"I can't explain it, Steve. You have to trust me. Life with Frank was too horrible to describe. He did beat me, but that was only a small part of it. It doesn't matter now." She laid her head on my shoulder, snuggled against me and sighed deeply. "All you need to know is that I love you and I love our family. The past is in the past. Okay baby?"

Although I had a million questions about why what she'd just told me and how it contradicted what she had told me initially, I believed that she had endured significant abuse and there was no way I could possibly understand what she'd been through.

I figured there was nothing to do but trust her; she needed comfort, not questioning. I put my arms around her. "Okay," I said. The situation was beyond my ability to comprehend, much less fix. "As long as you're okay with this. They're your kids. It's up to you."

After that, Mary just disappeared from our lives. Angie never mentioned her again, and I was afraid to ask.

—·—

I knew my relationship with Angie wasn't exactly healthy. I knew she stretched the truth, and sometimes outright lied, but I was so swayed by the idea of home and family that I looked the other way. I felt responsible for her, and also for little Jodi, who now viewed me as her father. How could I abandon them? They needed me.

I chose not to argue with Angie when her responses and her stories stopped making sense. It was futile because she was always able to prove her point. I avoided fighting in order to keep my family intact.

I didn't make the right decision.

Angie and I had known each other for about eight months when my house sold and it was time to move. I told Angie and Jodi that our new home would be a little mill house in a town called Kannapolis, a mill town, home of Cannon Mills and made famous by NASCAR driver Dale Earnhardt.

I left my job as a bread man, and purchased the rights to a personal hygiene vending business called Decorum which encompassed the whole state of North Carolina. I loved the idea of being my own boss, even though I knew I'd have to start from zero to build my customer base.

I left for North Carolina with high hopes for a happy future with my new family.

CHAPTER 3
NOTHING COULD BE FINER

TWO MONTHS LATER, Angie and I were married at the Cabarrus County Courthouse with my mom and my sister as witnesses. It was a wonderful way to be reunited with my mom, now widowed, and my sister. Mom was happy to welcome a daughter-in-law into the family, and she loved her new step-grandchild, Jodi. The dream of a happy family was turning into a reality.

I flew to Minnesota for training and learned more about Decorum. The company had begun selling only condoms in vending machines, but was now expanding their line to include things like feminine hygiene products and toothbrushes. While I was not too keen on buying an undeveloped sales route, I received encouraging estimates of projected sales for my North Carolina territory, which worked out to more than 1000 machines at about $500 per machine, minus product and equipment. This totaled over one million dollars, which almost sounded too good to be true.

Angie's brother Mike, rebounding from a failed marriage, needed a place to stay. I allowed him to move in with us, despite his horrible behavior at his mother's deathbed. So now we were four... Angie, Jodi, Mike and me. Our agreement was that Mike, while seeking employment, would do one household chore per day in lieu of paying rent. I handled the cooking, vacuumed and helped with the laundry; Mike was in charge of the dishes.

We continued with this system for several months, even after he got a job delivering for a medical supply company.

That fall it was time for Jodi to begin school. Angie had taken care of all the paperwork related to the registration in advance and asked me to go with them on the first day. As we walked up the front steps of the school, Jodi started crying and clung to her mom. Angie kept telling her that she had to go which only served to make Jodi cling more. Angie pried her off and then Jodi grabbed my leg.

I picked her up and held her for about two minutes (which seemed like a lifetime) and while she calmed down I told her, " Jodi, you're going to have fun with a whole bunch of kids who are just like you."

She calmed down and asked if we would go inside with her. I carried her to the class and for a few minutes we watched the kids playing. Jodi was still very hesitant. And after a few minutes I said, "Look, they're all waiting for you. Once you get in there, that's when they're really going to start playing, so you better hurry!"

"Are you going to come back for me?" she asked.

"Of course! You're my little girl!"

She went into the classroom and started playing with a little girl there. All was good so we left.

Once we got back into the car, Angie was all over me. "Oh my God, you are the best dad!"

Jodi came home that afternoon as happy as could be, telling us about her new friend. She was glad to go back the next day, and every day after that.

Soon after this, Angie became pregnant. Although her actions sometimes confused me and I didn't yet love her the way a man should love his wife, I was overjoyed at the prospect of becoming a father. My business was off to a strong start, our home was reasonably stable, and I'd always wanted a child of my own.

Our son Steven Mario Tenaglia was born on July 28, 1998. What an amazingly wonderful event this was! God blessed me with a beautiful, healthy, redheaded, blue-eyed little boy who triggered an awesome transformation within me. I was overwhelmed with the sense of love and responsibility I felt for this precious little baby, and I even began to feel, if not love for Angie, a deep respect and indebtedness to her for giving me such a gift. I was in awe of her, and also in awe of the special bond she seemed to display every time she was near our beautiful little boy. To me, she appeared almost angelic when she held him and nursed him.

Though my son was christened Steven, he quickly earned the loving nickname of Chub, because he was one plump baby. During the first few months of Chub's life, love ran rampant through our home, with my mom and my sister bonding with Angie and Jodi in such a way that my new family and my old family became one big happy family. I had never seen my mother and sister laugh and smile so much.

Life had become incredibly beautiful, filled with love, family and home. Little Steven's every move and sound enchanted me; even his cries sounded like music. In the deepest part of myself, I asked God daily that I might be good enough for this blessed gift.

—·—

But some darkness hovered around the edges. Months passed and while Angie kept a close eye on Chub, her attention was more like that of like a babysitter. Gone was the maternal love I'd witnessed when he was first born. With each passing day she seemed to become more and more distant, allowing my mother and sister to do the majority of the kissing, cooing, playing and nurturing that women tend to do with babies.

Angie had also become distant with me, but I'd heard that this sometimes happens in marriages immediately after a baby is born, so I let it go.

I wondered about what kind of mother she might be to little Steve, recalling when Jodi had choked on a penny. I had some concerns, so I watched her carefully. I could see that she took good care of the kids in a physical sense, making sure they were fed, bathed and supervised. But she wasn't expressing any emotion. She didn't smile, laugh or show joy and love.

Then her brother Mike's drug habit resurfaced, supported by the money he earned from his delivery job. He was still not paying rent, and it was clearly time for him to leave. When he neglected to do the dishes one night — his one and only chore — things went downhill quickly.

He had stopped talking to any of us, and spent all his time out with his friends or in his room. Angie agreed that it was time for him to go.

I confronted him in his room and said, "Mike, if one chore a day is too much, you're going to have to leave. And I will not have drugs or alcohol in my house, because there are children here."

He said he'd move as soon as he could find an apartment.

That conversation went far easier than I thought it would, and about a week later Mike found a place to live. Angie and I helped him move, and soon after, he fell in love with a girl named Anna, who had two little daughters. Mike tried to create a life with her, but soon lost his job due to his drug habit.

Mike moved back to Baltimore to live with his sister Dorothy. He stayed in touch with Anna and they made plans to reunite after he'd saved some money and got back on his feet. He found a job and managed to save up several thousand dollars to help him return to Anna and her little girls. He was hopeful about his new life, but then, out of the blue, we received the news that he had died from a drug overdose.

My mom looked after Jodi and Chub while Angie and I went to Baltimore for the funeral.

Dorothy said her brother had died after mixing Valium and beer.

In the back of my mind I thought something didn't sound quite right. I'm no pharmacist, but I was pretty sure that a person can't die from Valium and beer, especially someone like Mike, who was used to far more serious drugs. While we were at Dorothy's house, I noticed a prescription bottle on a bedside table. I slipped the bottle into my pocket and took it to the coroner's office the next day to ask if this medication had been found in Mike's system. They declined to say. I sensed there was much more to this story, so I went to the police and asked if Mike's death could be treated as a homicide. I strongly suspected that Dorothy had a hand in her brother's death. The police told me that the case was closed and had been ruled a suicide. I asked if they could re-open it and please check, and they declined.

Why did I suspect Dorothy? Because I knew that Mike had saved up at least $2000 in cash and that as a drug addict herself, Dorothy would have wanted to get her hands on that money. In Mike's truck we found many expensive gifts that he'd been planning to take to Anna and her daughters, but the cash was nowhere to be found.

Angie and her sister argued bitterly about the missing money. Angie accused her of killing Mike. The look on Dorothy's face as she slammed the door in our faces was a look of triumph, completely lacking any sorrow over her brother's death.

We started the seven-hour drive back to North Carolina and I cried for Mike while Angie, in what I thought must be a state of shock, sat staring blankly out the window.

"What kind of person is your sister?" I asked Angie.

"She's a slut. Dorothy was always jealous of me and always stole my boyfriends. She always had at least two boyfriends at one time, and she had two sons by two different men. She named her first son after the second boyfriend, and her second son after the first boyfriend."

This wasn't the answer I had expected, but I didn't know how to probe further. There were so many missing pieces to Angie's life story. She had never talked much about her parents or her childhood, but I had learned that she and her five siblings had survived abuse and trauma, and that their mother had been far from a model parent.

"Let it go, Steve. We're here now, together and in love," Angie said and put her hand over mine. "Dorothy doesn't matter. The past doesn't matter."

But the past did matter to me, and it was extremely troubling.

I had witnessed both Mike and Dorothy stealing their mother's pain medication while she was dying in the hospital, and now it looked like a reasonable possibility that Dorothy had killed Mike.

CHAPTER 4
DIPS IN THE ROAD

AFTER MIKE'S FUNERAL, the love of baby Steve and seven-year-old Jodi helped with the process of grieving. It caused me to think about Mary and I wondered how she was doing with Frank, but when I asked Angie, she evaded the question. She'd cut off contact with Frank, and showed no further interest in her older daughter.

Angie had been hired at KMart in Concord and I was busy trying to get a new business off the ground.

My first year with Decorum was a learning curve. I called the home office in Minnesota every day to learn where and how to install vending machines, while trying to ignore the less than savory reputation of the company. Although at first I had feared I had made a mistake buying into the operation, time, experience and the support of the company allowed my sales to go from zero to about $10,000 the first year. The company began testing many new products and I saw a good future in this business.

Trouble reared its head when Angie was accused of hitting her boss at KMart. She claimed he'd made a crude sexual advance toward her. It was her word against his and subsequently she lost her job. A week later, however, she got a new job working for K-Stores.

Our life settled into a normal routine with Jodi in school, Angie and I with our regular work schedules, and Steve keeping my mom, the doting grandmother, happily occupied. I left for work each morning and eagerly bustled through the day so I could come home to my family as early as possible. I spent the weekends enjoying time with the children.

Jodi was deeply attached to me, I was deeply attached to Chub, but Angie didn't seem to be attached to any of us. She went about the daily business of caring for the kids, but it seemed automatic. She became more and more withdrawn. I sensed something was wrong but had no idea what it could possibly be.

I tried many things to cheer her up. I even bought her a new, cherry red 1998 Pontiac Grand Am GT. While that improved the mood around the house for awhile, soon she was back in the dumps, complaining that she didn't feel good about herself any more. Since having the baby, she decided breast implants were necessary to make her feel pretty again. I obliged.

Then my brother Jerry got out of jail. Again.

A 6'-2", brown-haired, blue-eyed, charismatic guy, Jerry had once been athletic, but now he was an out of shape, drug-addicted alcoholic. His criminal history had begun with stealing my car when he was 15 years old. (In an attempt to get away, he ripped out his teeth and part of his bottom gum, getting them caught on the car mirror.) After that, he developed a drug habit, and had been accused of beating at least three women. At age 19, had was involved with a 51-year-old woman, whom he assaulted, slamming her head against the walls of her home. She'd moved to Florida to get away from him, but Jerry had followed her there.

In Florida, he found a job at a lumber yard, but he continued his drinking and crack cocaine habits. At one point he robbed a convenience store and hit a police officer while under the influence of alcohol and narcotics. He called Mom to bail him out of jail and get him out of Florida. She arranged for him to move to North Carolina. For nine years, my mom and my dad, who was crippled from a massive stroke, had allowed Jerry to live in their basement. During those years, Jerry worked odd jobs, smoked pot daily, and bragged about all the women he'd slept with. In a fit of rage, he threw a three-year-old across a room and broke the child's leg. Around the time I'd moved to North Carolina, he was arrested again for assaulting a female. After his release, he moved back into Mom's basement.

Comparing my life with Jerry's and the lives of Angie's siblings, I considered myself pretty lucky. I had a job, a house, a wife, stepdaughter, and little Steve.

— · —

One day after work, around two or three in the afternoon, when Steve was eight months old, I walked through the kitchen door and an awful stench hit me in the face. It seemed to be coming from the living room where Angie was feeding Steve.

"Angie, what's that smell?"

She said, "I don't smell anything."

"You've got to! It smells like something's gone bad."

She shrugged and continued to spoon food into little Steve's mouth.

I approached her and the baby, sniffing around to find the source of the terrible odor. "Angie, what are you feeding him?"

"Mashed bananas."

I picked up the little Heinz jar and almost gagged. It smelled like a rotting carcass. It did not look like mashed bananas, either. It was dark, a burnt orange color.

"Angie, there's something wrong with this food. Look at it. Look at the color! Smell it!"

"I don't smell anything."

Usually Angie's senses were very acute. She was always the first to notice unusual smells. She also had perfect vision and perfect hearing. It made no sense that she could be so close to this jar of rotten food and not smell it, since I had smelled it the second I had walked in the door.

The next morning Chub woke up irritable, crying and feverish. He had developed a severe diaper rash, and after he was fed, he would throw up whatever he'd just eaten. Angie took him to the pediatrician while I was at work. The doctor gave Chub a dose of Maalox and advised Tylenol for the fever.

Chub remained ill, with a fever and nausea, and then blisters developed on top of the diaper rash. We decided to take him to the local emergency room instead of going back to the pediatrician.

As the ER doctor examined Chub from head to toe, I told him about the baby food. He asked for more details about the food, so I went home to gather the information.

We had about eight jars of Heinz baby food left in the cupboard, and I called the 800 number on the label. I told someone at Heinz my story and they said they'd send someone to the house immediately to get the jars for testing.

A man and a woman from Heinz showed up within a couple of hours. They were very defensive, demanding to know what other foods my son had recently eaten, trying to fix the blame on something else, and acting more like cops than food manufacturers. I gave them all eight jars, and they assured me that they would contact me with the results.

My son recovered, but two things really bothered me. Though I kept calling Heinz, I never got answers. Ultimately, the manager at the store where we'd purchased the food told me that Heinz had come and had removed all the jars from the store.

The second thing that bothered me was Angie's reaction. There was no physical reason why she wouldn't have been able to smell the bad food. She didn't have a cold or any sinus problems, and her sense of smell was working just fine. Also, Chub had been eating mashed bananas for months, and they were always pale yellow. How could she have not noticed that the food in this jar was the wrong color?

When it was all over and Chub was well again, I asked her these questions and all she'd say was, "He's okay now isn't he? So it doesn't matter. Let it go."

And I did. I let it go, just like I let go of hundreds of other things.

Little Steve turned one and the four of us went to my mom's. It was a joy to see my mom so happy. I stood by and watched my mom and sister kiss my little boy over and over with the excuse, "It's his birthday!"

—·—

Over the next year or two, I gained more accounts for my Decorum business, and by paying close attention to the market, my sales rose more than five times by the end of my second year. While I was doing better with the business, I was losing control of my household.

My brother Jerry, still living in Mom's basement, spent a lot of time hanging out at my house. One day after work Jodi said, "I saw Mommy and Uncle Jerry kissing behind the garage."

Angie overheard and accused her of making it up, but Jodi argued back, insisting that she was telling the truth. Angie bullied Jodi into submission while my brother stood there and allowed Jodi to be subjected to her mother's tirade. I asked Jerry to leave, and for the rest of the night the argument continued, with Jodi crying, "But I *did* see you kissing Uncle Jerry," and Angie telling her to shut up and stop lying.

After she put her daughter to bed, Angie cuddled up to me and said, "You know, Jodi is just a kid, and kids make up stories. Of course I wasn't kissing Jerry. Why would I do something to hurt you and our beautiful family? You know how much I love you. I would never even look at another man."

I wanted to believe her.

About a week later, on the way home from work, I stopped to get gas. Angie's Grand Am was across the street at another gas station. I walked over and found my two-year-old son alone in the back seat. Jodi was apparently inside the convenience store, and Angie was some distance away leaning into another car, talking to a man with a rebel bandana tied around his head. When she saw me, she walked over, and the other car sped off.

"Why did you leave the baby alone in the car?" I asked.

"They asked me for directions to the mall."

It didn't make sense that someone five cars behind her in line for gas would have asked her anything, but I was more concerned that she'd left our son alone in the car. "I don't care what anyone asks you. You should never leave Steve alone in the car!"

Jodi came out of the store then. Angie told her to get in the car and they drove off. I filled my car and followed them home, arriving to find my brother there as well.

Since the kissing accusations, I didn't like him anywhere near Angie. I asked her to go into the bedroom with me to talk.

"Why were you leaning into that car?"

"Don't accuse me. Nothing happened!" She was clearly upset. "You're acting like a jealous jerk. I'm not doing anything I'm not supposed to be doing."

She was right. I *was* jealous. I suspected something was going on with Jerry, and now I suspected something was going on with the guy in the car at the gas station, too.

Jodi walked into the room, and not wanting to fight in front of her, I let it go. I figured I must be imagining things because Angie had defended herself with such conviction.

The next day I went to her workplace to apologize. When I walked in, I saw a guy that looked familiar, and as soon as he saw me, he turned and quickly left. What made him look so familiar was the rebel bandana on his head. It was the same guy from the gas station. "Who was that?" I asked.

"What are you accusing me of now?" Angie asked. "This is my job. You can't walk in here and interrupt me while I'm working."

"You're right," I said. "Maybe we can talk about this at home."

Of course, we never did. The incident got swept under the rug just like everything else.

CHAPTER 5
IT'S JUST BUSINESS

THE SUMMER OF 2000, aside from my suspicions about my wife's behavior, was a beautiful time in my life. God had blessed me with a beautiful, healthy and inquisitive son. As my little Steve ran and jumped and laughed and played, he was such a joy to watch. He was a handful for Angie, Jodi, and me to keep up with, too.

When he turned two, Steve really came into his own. Angie and I filled the kitchen with balloons for his birthday and my mom, sister and brother joined us for ice cream cake. As we sang "Happy Birthday," Angie wiped ice cream from Steve's mouth.

"Angie, don't worry about it! Leave a little ice cream on his face," Mom said, "He looks cute."

When he heard the word cute, little Steve began hamming it up, realizing that it was *his* party! He put down his spoon and plunged his face right into the cake. We were surprised at just how sweet a kid could look with ice cream dripping down his chin. With every bite came more laughter and so he hammed it up more. Diving down, grabbing a bite, and then popping up laughing hysterically, ice cream dripping — best birthday ever.

— . —

Angie and I settled into the routine of a regular married couple, and after the close call with Jerry and the guy in the car, she remained on her best behavior. She lavished flattery on me, kept the house spotless, held down a job and did her best to be an ideal wife and mother. There was nothing I wanted more than a happy family. Whenever Angie, the kids, and I would meet at Mom's house, it seemed like every day was Thanksgiving. I clung to every moment of happiness I could find.

Though she was working hard, Angie remained distant. Her vibrant, exuberant personality had all but disappeared. I asked her constantly if she was okay, and she assured me that everything was fine. Sometimes she'd tell me that her job was very demanding and she was tired, so I made a more conscious effort to help with the chores around the house. I believed what she said about her job, because she was a hard worker and always got a raise when it was time for a job evaluation. I knew that women who work full-time jobs while managing homes and children can easily get burned out, and I wanted to make things better for her.

One day I was supposed to meet with a Decorum client, but the meeting got cancelled, so I was home earlier than usual. I waited for Angie to get home after picking up the kids from my mom's, but when she pulled into the driveway about an hour earlier than usual, she was alone.

"Where are the kids?" I asked.

"I got finished with work early, and my boss is on his way over to review some paperwork that's required for my promotion," she said on her way into the house.

Just as she said that, a black Ford pickup pulled into our driveway. Angie's boss, Morrie, came out of his truck wearing skin-tight shorts and a belly shirt — not work attire. Angie ran toward the driveway, saying she would be right back. She spoke briefly with him, and within a minute he was gone. I asked Angie why he had to leave so quickly, and she told me he had a softball game and would discuss the paperwork with her the following day at work.

— · —

Business was robust and I decided to invest more in my route. I took out a loan for $100,000 to buy more machines and more products. Soon after that, Decorum, the company that I worked for, was sold. I learned major changes were on their way. Instead of my operating as a franchise where I owned my route, all the sales would now be managed at the corporate level; there would be no more independent owner/operators. The bottom line was that I was making such good money they realized *they'd* make more money if they didn't have any franchisees.

I stood to lose a small fortune. I asked if I might be able to sell out. The rep told me to be careful, and if I did sell, I should make sure to get cash for my business.

About a week later, four of my machines were vandalized. I called the company to let them know what had happened, and found that I had a new representative. When I explained the damage was both to my machines and to the product, he just laughed and said, "Get insurance."

I'd been led to believe that the machines were insured by Decorum and therefore, I didn't need to carry my own policy. The company had also guaranteed that the machines were tamper proof.

Shortly after that, the newest and most lucrative machine I had, a weight machine, was stolen. It had cost me about $1,200 and had more than $1,000 in quarters inside. A mall security camera pointed right at it, but when I reported it to mall security, nothing was done. It seemed like an inside job. Not only did mall security ignore my reports, I also reported it to the Concord Police Department five separate times, and nothing was ever done.

About a week later, my new Decorum representative asked if I would buy and service a company route on the east coast of North Carolina. Even though I already had all of the state, this route was apparently being serviced by someone else, and now they wanted to sell it back to me. He gave me all the reports on the route, and I agreed to the deal. After I had acquired the rights to the whole state I discovered Decorum was continuing to do business with this route through its sister company *Serve-Now*.

I asked why Decorum was running a business on the east coast of the state. "I bought the rights to the *whole* state."

My new rep said, "Does it matter?"

"Of course it matters. I bought the rights to the whole state, and you're running a competing business in my territory!"

None of this made any sense to me, but to keep myself employed, I bought them out of the route I'd just purchased, spending an additional $13,000 in the process. A few days later, adding insult to injury, my representative called to say that my credit was cancelled. A week after that, Decorum's rival company pulled into my driveway with 30 of my machines.

The keys to the machines had been given back to Decorum. My machines had been opened, removed from the walls in every retail outlet where I had installed them. I wanted to know how the competitor had gotten keys to my machines. I eventually learned that Decorum had actually sold my machines, claiming them as property of the company once my credit had been cancelled.

This effectively put me out of business. My rep suggested I sell out. "You have no more business," he said, "but we have a buyer for it."

A man named Darren Long called, offering to buy my business. We later met at my house and I agreed to sell at the end of the year. Although he seemed displeased, he agreed to my terms.

Mr. Long, the previous owner and founder of the company, wanted my route back because it was so lucrative. I'd been making $213,000 a year, and he wanted that profit for himself. In order to do this, he had done everything he could to crush me, including vandalizing my machines.

I was out of business.

CHAPTER 6
A LITTLE GET AWAY

THOUGH I SOON found another delivery job with a different company, the whole experience with Decorum had been exhausting. Angie said she needed a vacation. So did I. "Okay, where would you like to go, and when?" I asked.

"Anywhere!" she said. "And soon!"

I made reservations at a hotel at Myrtle Beach. Happy again, Angie went to work with new enthusiasm. She cleaned the house, and her exuberance toward the kids and me returned.

Angie and the kids were going to spend the week at the beach, and I planned to join them on the weekend. When I arrived, Jodi and Steve smothered me with love, and the hotel room was bursting with happiness, except for Angie, who was moody and withdrawn. Steve and Jodi regaled me with nonstop stories about their adventures at the beach, and then Jodi told me something that made me come down from my proud fatherly cloud.

"Today Mommy left Chub and me by the pool by ourselves, Dad."

"Why would you leave the kids alone by the pool?" I asked her.

Angie said, "I didn't leave the kids by the pool by themselves. She's making up stories again."

Jodi said, "Yes, you did, Mom!"

"I asked a lady to watch the kids while I ran up to the room to get my cigarettes."

"Did you know this lady?"

"Her kids were playing with our kids, and when I told her that I needed to run to up to our room, she said she would be happy to watch the kids."

End of conversation.

The next morning we went to McDonald's for breakfast. I took the kids to the playground section to play while Angie waited for our food. That's when I noticed a guy with funny-looking glasses staring at the kids. When Angie joined us I asked her, "Hey, is it me, or is that guy staring at us?"

Angie put the food on the table, and said, "What guy?"

While I was still staring at this guy, who made it very clear he was staring at us, I said, "That guy."

She finally looked up and the guy walked away and disappeared into the parking lot. Angie seemed completely unconcerned so there was no reason to press the issue.

The next two days were wonderful. I had fun with my two beautiful kids running along the beach and playing in the pool. But all that running in the sand and splashing in the surf was more than my 5'-8'', 225-pound body could handle, so I vowed to go on a diet and get into "kids" shape. (When we returned home, I bought a Soloflex weight machine and set it up in the garage.)

We left the coast and headed home, a five hour trip. Angie had Chub because she had the car seat, and Jodi rode with me. We arrived home with two sleeping kids and a week's worth of sandy laundry.

While lying in bed that night, I asked Angie, "So how was that vacation."

"All right."

"Just all right?"

"What do you want me to say?"

"You were there the whole week with the kids, and I just wanted you to share with me what I missed."

"You didn't miss anything. I need to get some sleep."

I was disappointed, but knew she must be tired. We both had to go to work the next day and I let the matter drop.

Angie was now getting up for work as early as I did, around one a.m. She'd dress the kids, and put them, still sleeping, into the car for the 12-mile ride to my mom's house. I usually got home around three o'clock in the afternoon, getting home to the kids as soon as I could. My brother Jerry was still hanging around, and I helped him find a job loading trucks for a company where I'd worked while starting my business.

As I got more accustomed to my new job, I was able to get home a little earlier every week, until I arranged my schedule such that I got home around noon. I'd have lunch with Angie and Steve, and Jerry would stop by every day around three to talk about his new job. The kissing incident was totally forgotten.

CHAPTER 7
UNFINISHED BUSINESS

IN EARLY 2001, Darren Long and I met again to finalize the sale of my business. I suggested that we discuss the terms of the sale and then have attorneys draw up a contract. He said there was no need to pay for lawyers; he was a CPA and could easily handle the transaction.

He asked how much I wanted for the business.

I had done my homework. "Businesses such as mine typically sell for two to three times gross annual sales, plus the value of the machines," I said.

"But you don't have a business anymore.

"Excuse me, I'm doing over $200,000 in sales, and I am asking 2.75 times my yearly sales.

"IF you did $212,000, let's keep the numbers round and figure I'll do $200,000. That sound fair?"

I supposed so.

"So," he said and punched some numbers in his calculator. "Looks like 2.75 times 200,000 equals 202,000." He turned his calculator around and showed me the number.

"That doesn't seem right," I said.

"You saw me do it."

"It's a lot more than that."

He punched in the numbers again and showed me the same number:

202,000.

He pulled some paperwork from his briefcase and asked me to sign and initial.

"I don't agree with your math," I said.

"It's this, or nothing."

He proposed paying me half up front (which I owed to the bank) and the balance over four quarters, interest free. When I didn't immediately agree, he threatened again to pay nothing at all.

When I got home, I used my calculator and ran the numbers. My math showed that my business was actually worth $550,000, plus the value of my machines, worth about $100,000. In addition, there was value added due to four years of my labor, installing and maintaining the machines.

When we met again the following day, I told him the actual value of my business was closer to $750,000. He refused to offer more than $303,000.

My breakeven point was $325,000.

I left his office beaten and humiliated.

Though I had obtained another job, it wasn't great and I threw myself into finding a new opportunity. Soon, I had a new job as an owner/operator for a bakery. I was happy to be a breadman again.

CHAPTER 8
SHADOWS

LIFE TURNED AROUND. Angie appeared to be less depressed. The kids were healthy and happy. My brother had a job and seemed relatively stable. And I was getting home at an acceptable hour, doing what I'd done in Baltimore.

Every day, my mom gave me full reports on everything that the kids did. She was grateful that I had helped my brother get a job and I was thankful for her watching the kids and getting Jodi to school every day.

Everything seemed as though it was as good as it could get. We were solidly part of the middle class; we had jobs; we were paying our bills; and living a good life with two beautiful children.

With decent jobs and a house that was now paid off, I decided it was time to move to a nicer neighborhood. Angie and I started looking for a new house in Concord, a larger town a few miles away, which was closer to our jobs and where the schools were highly-rated.

Then things became a little less perfect. Darren Long had been making his quarterly payments, but midway through 2002, he decided not to pay the last $110,00, claiming that I had refused to help him with business issues in South Carolina. I hired an attorney. It looked as if it would be twelve months before I could have my day in court.

My brother continued to stop by on his way to work, and after about two weeks at his new job, he came by with a six-pack of beer. I told him that I didn't want any drinking in my house, and not only that, he should not drink and drive, not to mention going to work with beer on his breath.

Within a day or two after asking my brother not to drink in my house, Angie offered me a vodka and cranberry juice while she had a rum and Coke. When I asked her what was up with the drinking all of a sudden, she told me, "I love you and I want to celebrate all the good things in our lives."

I said that a drink every once in a while couldn't hurt. But I really preferred not to have alcohol in the house.

The next day Angie was happy and full of enthusiasm. We were playing happily with the kids when there was a knock at the door. It was Jerry, holding another six-pack, and he was drunk.

"Jerry," I said, "you're not welcome here when you're drinking."

"Don't give me that hypocritical bullshit." he said. "You and Angie were drinking yesterday. "

The only way Jerry could know that Angie and I had a drink together was if she'd told him.

"You drink," he said in a drunken rage, "but you don't want me to drink."

I told Jerry to go sleep it off in the spare bedroom. I called his job and told them he was sick. After about five hours he got up. Although he screamed and yelled and continued to act like a jerk, he was sober enough to drive. He took his beer and went home.

One day that summer I noticed cigarette butts outside, under one of the bedroom windows. I didn't pay much attention to it. I just cleaned it up, figuring the butts probably belonged to the yard guy. Then a couple of nights later I got a phone call from the neighbor across the street telling me that there was a man hanging around my garage. I ran outside, telling Angie to call 911.

I saw a man down the street and hollered at Angie to throw me my keys. When I got into my truck to go after him, Angie came to the door and yelled, "Don't hurt him!"

I caught up with him seconds later. Jumping out of the truck, I grabbed him just as the police pulled up. I explained what happened and they took him into custody.

Had this man been standing beside my house smoking his cigarettes while he watched my family?

This made me even more determined to find a new house. Angie said she'd never seen him before.

A few nights later, about midnight, my brother came knocking at our front door. He was drunk again and screaming, "I beat that old bastard, and I beat him bad."

Confused and half asleep, I said, "What are you talking about?"

"You know the old man that works as a guard? Well I beat him, I stomped him, and I kicked his ass."

I told Jerry to go to bed and sleep it off.

He kept bragging, "I stomped him, I stomped him."

Less than an hour later, there was another knock at my door. This time it was the police, with their guns drawn. They asked if Jerry was in the house, and I said, "Yes, but no guns in the house, please. I have two kids." They entered my house, guns holstered, and arrested my brother.

One of the officers said that an altercation at Jerry's workplace had escalated. Supposedly, the guard, reputed to be a pretty cocky older man in his seventies, hadn't opened the security gate fast enough to suit some of the workers. One word led to another and my brother hit him. Jerry had beaten the guard so brutally that the man was in critical condition.

I called Mom.

"Dear God," Mom sobbed. "I feel so bad for that poor man and his wife. Dear God, I am so sorry."

"I'm sorry, too, Mom."

I just hoped the man would be okay; but at his age, it would be hard to recover easily or completely. "We have to pray, Mom," I said. "We have to pray for that man and his family."

Three days went by before we found out that the man my brother had beaten was expected to recover. Jerry was charged with felony assault. At my mom's insistence, Angie and I bailed Jerry out of jail. Mom paid for his lawyer. Jerry was found guilty and sentenced to a year in jail.

CHAPTER 9
JOYS & SORROWS

ANGIE AND I SOLD our little house and moved in with my mom for about six months while we looked for the ideal house. Hoping to be out of my mom's house before Jerry got out of jail, I found a house just beyond our financial means in a beautiful little town called Mt. Pleasant, near Concord. We moved into our new house in September, 2002.

At the end of a cul de sac, on just under four acres, we found a ten-year-old, brick ranch with four bedrooms, two bathrooms and a two-car garage. Best of all, it had a 900 sq. ft. playroom and a twenty foot oval above ground pool surrounded by a full deck. Angie wasn't too keen about having a pool. She said she couldn't swim and was terrified of the water. Still it seemed like the perfect house for a family.

All that was missing was a dog.

We adopted Chelsea, a German shepherd mutt, when she was six weeks old. She was never put on a leash because if I were a dog, I certainly wouldn't want to be put on a leash. She understood our place was hers and she never wandered from home. She became my children's dog and their friend but most of all, she was their guardian.

To support our new lifestyle, it took both of our incomes.

We used the furniture from our first house, but we had to save up to buy furniture for the additional rooms. Among our first purchases was new bedroom furniture for Jodi. We got her a white canopy bed and outfitted it with a white ruffled comforter and pretty sheets. She loved it, and looked just like a princess tucked in her new bed at night.

It should have been an exciting, happy time, but Angie grew depressed again. When I'd ask what was wrong, she'd simply tell me she had a lot on her mind.

I wasn't only concerned about her depression. In addition to working all the time —seven days a week — Angie began to exhibit reckless behavior, especially when driving. Driving her Pontiac, she'd push the driver's seat all the way back, stick her left foot out the window, and turn the radio up to full volume, even with the kids in the car.

Because of this, I tried to limit the amount of time she spent alone with the kids. But I really enjoyed spending time with them, so it was not a hardship to hurry home from work every day and play with them in our quiet little neighborhood.

Not surprisingly, around this time Angie had a car accident, just a little fender bender, on her way home from work. The reason: distracted driving. A couple of good Samaritans helped her out and there was no need report the incident. I hoped this would cause her to straighten up and take being behind the wheel more seriously. Maybe for awhile it did.

Then, a second tattoo appeared, this time on her ankle—a teddy bear holding two balloons. I was suspicious. I asked her what it represented.

"I don't have to tell you," she said.

Angie's behavior left me increasingly confused, making me feel off-balance almost constantly. I found myself working out more and more frequently, using the Soloflex weight machine in the garage as a way to blow off steam. It was the best way I could calm down.

—·—

I always had a little extra inventory that I was free to share with friends and family. Little Steve loved to help open the doors to my bread truck when I got home and fill his little toy wagon with bread and cakes. We hitched his wagon to his tricycle and he'd make his own deliveries around the neighborhood, Chelsea by his side. Jodi and Steve would play until about five o'clock, and then when Angie got home, the four of us would usually go to my mom's house for dinner.

After dinner, the kids might ride their bikes for a little bit, then have their baths and watch a little television before their eight o'clock bedtimes. Every night, Steve would run into our bedroom to hug and kiss his mom. "Good night, Mommy," he'd say. "I love you." I'd laughingly try to pull him away, which of course made him hug Angie all the harder.

Steve liked me to massage his toes and work my way up to the top of his head. First he'd say, "Rub." And then after I made it up to his scalp, he'd say, "Okay, Dad, can you tuck me in now?"

Every day felt like a blessing. There were no more stalkers, Jerry was out of our hair for the time being, and the status quo held steady into early fall.

I couldn't have been happier. Angie, however, remained distant from our family activities.

— · —

Jodi's school was hosting a Halloween party the last Friday of the month, and she wanted to go as a vampire. I volunteered to take her shopping for her costume on Wednesday, my day off. When I got home from work that day, Angie was asleep on the couch and said she was too tired to go with us. I collected Steve from pre-school and then Jodi after her school let out.

When we got to the store, Steve, once he grasped the concept of Halloween and costumes, decided that he wanted to be a clown and grabbed a colorful little clown outfit.

"Why do you want to be a clown, Chub?" I asked. Personally, I didn't think being a clown was the best choice for my little boy. I was hoping for something a little more macho.

He looked at me with a *don't-you-understand?* look, and said, "Because I wanna make everybody happy, Dad!"

Wow! I was ashamed of myself. Who cares about macho?

He made me so proud. Here was a good little person who had so much to teach the rest of us. I had never realized the special gifts of kindness and joy one little boy could share with others. Of course I bought him a flaming red wig and all the make-up necessary to make his costume complete.

Friday, the day of Jodi's Halloween party, I got home to find Angie asleep again. I shut the bedroom door and left to go pick up Steve from preschool. As I sat in my SUV, I watched my son on the playground pushing other kids on the swings. I vowed not to allow Angie's lack of enthusiasm ruin our Halloween spirit. And I vowed to spend my life not just as a good person, but as the very best person I could possibly be, because I was a role model for my little boy, even though *he* was the one teaching *me* a lot about life.

When school let out Steve came running full speed into my arms. "Hey, Dad! Where's Mommy?"

"Mommy's sleeping. Were you a good boy in school today?"

He smiled and said, "Of course, I was Dad. When we get home can I wear my clown outfit?"

"Of course you can son," I said, but knowing his mother was home sleeping I thought it was best to delay getting home. "First, let's go get some ice cream."

We got some ice cream cones and when we drove into the drive, Chelsea, our now 60-pound German shepherd, bounded up to us. Steve promptly dropped his ice cream, and Chelsea promptly devoured it.

I expected tears. Instead, Steve looked down at his ice cream, then looked up at me and said, "It's okay, Dad, Chelsea likes ice cream, too."

Wow, I thought, *what a kid*.

We went inside and found Angie sitting in the kitchen. Steve ran to her and said, "Hi, Mommy! I missed you today."

She held him back and said, "Leave me alone, Chub."

He stopped, all his joy gone, replaced by disappointment.

"Don't treat him like that," I said. "Can't you see how much he loves you?"

Angie started screaming, "You fuckin' dick, I hate you and these fuckin' brats, I fuckin' hate you!"

Angie had had this kind of outburst before, but never so unexpectedly, and never directed at the kids.

I didn't care about the things Angie said to me. She could call me all the bad names in the world, but I could not bear for her to say such things in front of the kids. I quickly picked up Steve and took him into the garage. He had a look of horror on his face, and I said, "Chub, it's okay, Mommy doesn't feel well. Why don't you stay out here and play with Chelsea? Don't leave the garage, okay?"

"Okay, Dad. Is Mommy okay?"

"Yeah, Chub, but promise me you'll stay in the garage while I talk to Mommy."

I went back into the house and asked Angie, "What was that all about?"

"I hate you, you fuckin' dick. I hate my life."

She came at me swinging, punching with both fists, screaming, I backed up so I wouldn't get hit in the face, but she kept swinging and screaming, "I hate you and those fuckin' kids."

I didn't know what to say or do. "Why? What's wrong? Why are you doing this in front of Chub? Let's just talk about whatever it is."

She finally sat, still seething with anger,

Steve walked in, crying. He'd obviously heard everything his mother had said. My heart sank as I saw him standing there. I picked him up and held him until he could catch his breath.

"What's the matter with Mommy?" he asked. "Why is she hitting you?"

Angie yelled, "Dammit, leave me alone!" She went into the bedroom and slammed the door behind her.

I tried to divert my son's attention. "Hey, Chub, don't worry. Mommy's just tired, and sometimes grownups get grumpy when they're tired. I have an idea. Let's go to the park."

"I don't want to leave Mommy. Can we just stay here? I don't want to go to the park."

He was so worried about his mom that he turned down the park, which was completely out of character for him.

"OK, but let's be real quiet so we can let Mommy sleep."

We tiptoed through the hallway, but we could hear her talking on the phone.

"Mommy's awake!" Steve ran into our bedroom room and jumped on the bed.

Angie quickly said, "I've got to go," and hung up.

Little Steve wrapped himself around her, kissing her, and said, "I love you, Mommy. Are you okay?"

"Yes, Chub, I'm okay," she said as if the previous outburst had never happened. "I love you, too." Then Angie looked at me and asked, "I thought you were going out?"

"We were, but Chub was worried about you. He was so worried that he gave up the park for you. What on earth is wrong?"

A weird expression came over her as she pulled Chub close and kissed him on the mouth. I mean, she kissed him *hard* on the mouth, in an inappropriate way that lasted much longer than a mother/child kiss should last.

"What are you doing!?"

Angie, with an exaggerated look of innocence, asked, "What do you mean?"

"You know what I mean. Why did you kiss him like that? What are you thinking to kiss a kid that way?"

So she did it again, but this time, much more softly, but still, far too long. She looked at me defiantly and said, "Because I'm his mother, and that's how I want to kiss my baby. Right Chub? Mommy loves you."

It was all too strange... her violent outburst... the cell phone call with the quick "I've got to go,"... the inappropriate kiss. Now was not the time to confront her. Not in front of Chub; I didn't want to risk unleashing the monster that was swinging at me in the kitchen ten minutes earlier.

I reminded Angie that Jodi's Halloween party was that night and asked her to help me get Chub dressed in his costume.

When Steve heard me mention his costume, he squealed with happiness, "I'm gonna be a clown! I'm gonna be a clown!"

But Angie ignored him and said, "You get him ready. I'm busy."

"With what?"

"I have a lot of work tomorrow, and I have to get up early."

I looked at her and said, "Angie, you work seven days a week. What the hell are you doing that's so important? It's not like you're some big executive running a multi-million-dollar company. You work at K-Stores. This party is a big deal for Jodi, and it's more important than your job. Your family needs you."

She reluctantly helped me get our son dressed, and after about twenty minutes we had the cutest little clown in town. When he looked in the mirror, he screamed with joy, "I love my outfit! This is what I wanted to look like. I love you Dad!"

He jumped into my arms and gave me the hardest hug he could. I pulled my head back, looked at him and said, "What about Mommy?"

He ran over to Angie's lap in a blink, saying, "I love you too, Mommy! This is how I wanted to look! Wait till Jodi sees me!"

Angie said nothing. Her face was blank.

While Steve stood by the window waiting for Jodi's school bus to arrive, I attempted another conversation with Angie. It was the usual game of 20 questions, "Why were you so nasty to Chub? Why did you hang up the phone so fast?"

"It was work. Why are you so nosey?"

"Look, you're a stock girl. You're working seven days a week and now they're calling you at home? I don't think so. What's really going on?"

"See, there you go again. I can't talk to anyone without you butting in."

"I care about you and the kids, and that's why I try to talk to you about what's going on." I thought this might give me an in-road to an actual meaningful conversation, but at that moment, Steve ran into the kitchen shouting, "Jodi's here! I'm going to show her my clown outfit!"

I said, "Hey Chub, why don't you run to your room and hide behind your bed, and when Jodi comes in, you can surprise her."

"Okay Dad," he said and went running to his room.

"Angie," I said, "I'm just concerned about some of your behavior. Driving with the seat all the way back, your foot hanging out the window and the music blasting. It isn't safe."

"Who are you, my father?"

"No. I'm your husband and I care about your safety and I want our kids to be safe."

"Don't tell me what to do. You're not my father."

"Where is your father anyway? Why doesn't he have anything to do with you?"

"He tried to rape me once and I had him arrested."

Well, that put an end to the conversation. All I could say was that I was sorry. "Is there anything I can do?"

"Just leave me alone."

Jodi arrived and wanted to change right into her vampire costume. I said first she had to help Chub clean up his room. Mightily disappointed, she walked down the hall to Chub's room.

I heard him jump out from behind his bed and shout, "Look at me Jodi, I'm a clown!"

They both dissolved into laughter.

Jodi got dressed in her vampire costume, but decided to wait until after dinner to put on her make-up. Steve's makeup was already running down his face after all his running around.

We went to mom's house for dinner and she and my sister loved the kids' outfits. Jodi loved the attention and little Steve was really amped up. Angie was nervous and impatient the whole time.

When we stopped at home on the way to Jodi's party to refresh her costume, Angie went straight to bed. I now had the two revved up kids on my hands, and really could have used Angie's help. But she was not interested.

Chub begged me to let him go to the party with Jodi. He didn't understand that it was a party for older kids, and he was heartbroken and cried all the way home after we had dropped Jodi off at the party. He'd promised to be good, claimed he was a big kid too, and just didn't want to take no for an answer. I tried to bribe him with the promise of a candy bar and detoured two blocks to go to a convenience store.

As I parked, I said, "Hey, Chub, you can't let anyone see you cry You're a clown, right? Clowns don't cry. So come on, make everybody happy."

His tears stopped, but instead of a smile, I got a stubborn frown.

The smile showed up when the lady at the counter started talking to him. We hung out there for about twenty minutes, which took us to about eight o'clock and bedtime.

I carried Chub inside, and about 15 feet from the bedroom I heard Angie say, "I gotta go."

Chub ran into the bedroom and jumped onto the bed to greet his mother, and as they hugged, I looked at her and asked, "Who was on the phone?"

And as nice as could be, she said, "It was my job, and they want me to go in early tomorrow."

"Something real important must be going on at your job, for them to keep calling you."

"It's inventory tomorrow."

"Chub, run on to your room and I'll be there in a minute to tuck you in," I said. "You know Angie, it's after eight, and I've got work tomorrow, too. I've been running like a nut all day trying to keep up with the kids, and all you've done was yell, scream, curse, talk on the phone, and quickly hang up every time we get close."

"You fuckin' jerk. I told you, I have inventory in the morning."

I shot back, "I own and run a business, and I do inventory *every day*. Do I yell and curse at you, and then talk on the phone to someone, and then when you get close enough, do I hang up?"

And then I couldn't stand it anymore. "Are you seeing someone?"

She expertly switched gears from anger to kindness, and softly said, "Of course not. I love you and the kids. You are my life. I would never do anything to ruin what we have."

"Then why do you act so secretive when you're on the phone, and why do you yell and curse at me and the kids?"

And with that same look of exaggerated kindness, she softly said, "Because my job is really getting to me. I'm sorry. Just let me get caught up. I'll make it up to you and the kids tomorrow, but right now I have to go to sleep. It doesn't help that you're pressuring me all the time. I need some space, and your nagging only makes it worse."

Chub had fallen asleep, still dressed in his clown outfit. I called for Angie to come see how cute he was.

"I told you, I have to get up early for inventory at work tomorrow!"

CHAPTER 10
DOWNWARD SPIRAL

THE NEXT DAY, instead of doing inventory, Angie got fired. She had important business to take care of at work all right, but it had nothing to do with work.

She told me it was because she took too many cigarette breaks, but I suspected that wasn't true.

I stopped by K-Stores and learned that Angie was fired for stealing. Specifically stealing time. Angie was going in at two o'clock in the morning and in addition to punching her time card, she also punched her girlfriend Gail in. When Gail came in, she would get Angie's time card and punch Angie out when she left, long after Angie had already left for the day. When this was discovered, both Gail and Angie were fired.

Now our family had lost its health insurance and a second income.

I confronted her, but she insisted that she was fired for taking too many cigarette breaks.

I kept trying to make sense of it. I asked, "Angie, isn't it bad enough you lost your job for stealing, but now you have to lie about it?"

"WHO TOLD YOU?"

"Does it matter who told me? The fact is you lost your job for stealing. Why did you lie?"

She yelled — and lied — again, "I'm not lying. I didn't steal. I told you what happened."

It was impossible to argue with her. Normal two-way conversation was something that rarely happened with Angie.

It was time to go get Chub from preschool, so I put the conversation on hold.

But Angie was obsessed about who gave me the information about her getting fired. I told her to calm down and concentrate on getting another job. "Don't lie. And stop yelling at me. Just learn from the mistake you made, and do better."

I did not realize that to her, *doing better* meant to lie and cheat better.

A few days later, I came home from work and found my brother Jerry and Angie together in the garage. When I got within hearing range, it was clear that Jerry was drunk. He hollered at me, "Hey, Angie wants a divorce."

Angie left the garage and walked into the house. Jerry hollered again, but louder, "Get it asshole? She wants a divorce."

"Fine," I said. "I'll talk to her."

"She wants her own apartment. She doesn't love you. She wants out."

I went inside and found Angie in the kitchen. "What's he talking about?" I asked, "Do you want a divorce?"

"Of course I don't want a divorce. You know how your brother gets when he's drunk. He's just making shit up."

"You mean the same way Jodi was making shit up when she saw you two kissing?"

Jerry was still outside yelling. "She wants her own apartment. She doesn't want to live here."

I returned to the garage and told Jerry to leave. As he drove off, he was still screaming, "She wants her own apartment. She doesn't want to live with you."

I called Mom to tell her we weren't coming over for dinner. "I don't know what's going on. Jerry's drunk and screaming that Angie wants a divorce."

"I was looking forward to seeing you and the kids," Mom said. She sounded terribly disappointed and said she'd cooked a big meal. "How bad is your brother?"

"Drunk and stupid, as usual. I can't have that around the kids."

"His drinking has got to stop. This isn't fair to you, me, or the kids, not to mention anyone driving on the roads," Mom said.

After talking with Mom, I asked Angie, "Why did you let Jerry get drunk over here today? And what was he doing here anyway?" and then I asked her point blank, "Do you want a divorce?"

Angie looked at me in disgust and said, "Yes. I hate your fucking guts. I want to get away. I want to get away from you and the kids."

"Why? The kids love you. What's wrong?"

"I have no time to myself. You and the kids take all my time."

"What are you talking about? You have nothing *but* time to yourself now. You don't have a job but the kids are either at school or at my mom's. You sleep when you want, go out when you want, and lie to me all the time. You're as free as a bird. So what is so wrong?"

"Oh just forget it. All you do is badger me and accuse me. It's impossible to talk to you."

"Wait a minute." I followed her. "I'm not going to just forget it. Do you want a divorce or don't you?"

Then her characteristic mood change. "Of course I don't want a divorce, we have kids."

"Then why would my brother say that? And if we have kids and you don't want a divorce, why do you want to get away? Where do you want to go? Why won't you talk to me?

"Because you're a dick and you wouldn't understand. Just forget it. Let's go get Chub."

We went to get Chub and took her car. As usual, she had the driver's seat tilted so far back she was barely able to see over the steering wheel. I didn't say anything at first because I wanted to see how she was going to drive like that. She rolled the window all the way down and put her left foot out the window and started down the street.

I asked her, "How are you even going to turn left?"

"Are you going to tell me how to drive now?"

"Yes, I *am* gonna tell you how to drive," I said. Actually, she drove the seven mile distance pretty well, although she did drive about ten miles over the speed limit the whole way.

When we got to Steve's preschool I said, "Look, I don't want to argue over ridiculous things, but driving like that is stupid."

Before she could respond, our son came running out from school, his hands full of papers he'd worked on throughout the day. I buckled him into his car seat and he handed me his schoolwork. Stapled to the top of the stack was his Christmas wish list. It included: a train, a horn for his bike, and tracks for the train.

When we got home, Steve ran to his tricycle and said, "Dad, I want a horn for *this* bike!"

Angie went into the house, and I played for an hour with Steve.

—·—

One day I pulled into the driveway after work and I heard the stereo blasting. Inside, Angie was dancing like a stripper in front of Chub, sticking out her tongue, stroking her breasts, and grabbing her crotch.

I turned off the music. "You're out of control. What are you doing?"

She shrugged. "I was just dancing."

"Like a stripper. In front of your four-year-old son! You don't see anything wrong with that?" I was so upset I was shaking. Something was seriously wrong with this woman.

"I just lost my job and you don't even care!"

"Look, I do feel bad about you losing your job. I am embarrassed about *how* you lost your job. But you can't dance like that in front of our son. You're his *mother*."

"Dancing makes me feel better. It's just *dancing*. I'm not doing anything wrong." She picked up our son and he wrapped his arms around her and gave her a big kiss.

I stood there confused about how angry I had just been. Maybe I had overreacted. "I'm gonna take a nap," I said. It had been a long day and I was exhausted. "You got Chub?"

"Just go to bed."

I stretched out on the bed, but couldn't relax. I strained to hear Steve's voice and listened to him playing. After a few minutes, when I couldn't hear him any more, I jumped up and looked out the window. Outside, Steve's bike was in the street, but I couldn't see him.

I ran down the hall and into the garage. Steve was there playing with the dog. Angie was on the phone.

She saw me and hung up quickly. "I thought you needed to take a nap."

"I saw Chub's bike in the street and I was worried. I just wanted to make sure he was all right."

"You're checking up on me, not Chub."

"Who was on the phone?"

"None of your business. Go back to bed!"

The next day, to make amends, I stopped on the way home from work and bought a bouquet of flowers. Steve and Angie were outside playing when I pulled in the drive. Steve ran over to greet me and I told him I had some flowers. "What should we do with them, Chub?"

"I give the flowers to Mommy!" and he ran with the flowers to his mother. She picked him up and hugged him.

"I love you, Mom!"

Later, Angie told me she had been out looking for work. I was happy to hear this and told her as much. I hoped if she could find another position, things might even out and get back to normal.

The next day I came home from work to find my son screaming, "I not a fucking brat, Mommy. I not a fucking brat!"

He said, "Mommy keeps calling me a fucking brat, and I not a brat… I not a brat, Dad, I'm a good boy."

As he cried, I asked Angie, "Why are you doing this to him?"

She charged at me, swinging, saying, "I hate you, you motherfucker, I hate you."

Her breath reeked of alcohol.

She swung at me with such ferocity that I could feel the air move past my face. As I ducked, I could see Steve was horrified. I pushed Angie down onto the couch and said, "This has got to stop, what the hell is wrong with you? It's bad enough you act the way you do, but now you're tormenting the baby. And you're drunk! When did you start drinking during the day? Sleep it off. I'll take care of the kids. Just stay out of my sight"

I wiped the tears from Chub's face, collected the keys to all the vehicles, and took my son to the park. It took about an hour to get him back to his happy, little boy self. We went to meet Jodi's bus and I took them both to get ice cream. I was in no hurry to return home.

Thankfully, Angie was sleeping when we got back to the house. I helped Jodi with her homework while little Steve played video games. At eight o'clock I put the kids to bed.

It occurred to me that night that the kids were all I had.

—·—

A few days later, I stopped at home before my last delivery to check in. The kids were at my mom's house. Angie was drunk again.

She was a mess, her makeup was smeared and she looked terrible. I suggested that she pull herself together and clean up. While I went out to my truck to get my last order ready, I caught a glimpse of her leaving the house and heading down the road. I waited about ten minutes, and then followed in the truck.

I made my last delivery, then looped back, driving past a bar in Kannapolis. My brother's truck was in the parking lot. I figured he might know where Angie was, and stopped there to ask him. Jerry was not in the bar.

I walked across the parking lot to a motel and asked the manager for my wife by name. He told me she was in room 11.

My heart pounding, I knocked on the door. I could hear people scrambling around on the other side of the door. It felt like it took forever before the door opened, and finally, there stood my wife... and my brother. The room reeked of alcohol, and they were clearly both drunk. So drunk in fact, that my brother was falling over while struggling to get his pants on, and Angie had her shirt on backwards.

I stood there with my mouth hanging open and tears streaming down my face. I vaguely remember hearing Angie say, "We were just talking!"

"What's going on?"

"I'm so sick of you accusing me of shit. You're so damn controlling. Why did you follow me here?"

She said this as if *I* was the one who had done something wrong.

"Angie," I stammered, as calmly as I could. "Are you even remotely aware of what you're doing? You are in a motel room, drunk and half-dressed with my brother. Do you think I'm that stupid? I'm not a stupid man."

I turned to Jerry. "Does she know how many other filthy whores you've been with? And all the men you've had sex with in jail?"

Barely believing what was happening, I told Angie to get in my truck.

Angie kept saying, "Nothing happened, we were just talking."

"Then why was he putting his pants on? Why is your shirt on backwards? If you wanted to talk, you could have done that anywhere, you didn't need a motel room."

When we got to Mom's house Angie waited in the truck while I went in to get the kids. Mom could see how upset I was, and I did not hesitate to tell her that I'd just found Jerry in bed with Angie at a motel.

I collected the kids, got back in the truck and drove my broken family home.

It took all the strength I could muster to put on a happy face while putting the kids to bed. When they were settled, I walked into my bedroom, where I found Angie passed out on her stomach...naked.

"Get up," I said. "Wash my brother's stink off you."

She rolled over and I was shocked to see her pubic hair had been shaved.

I knew exactly what that meant. "You *did* fuck my brother! He makes all his whores shave their pussies! You lying bitch!"

I wanted to punch something, *someone*. Angie, Jerry, the wall... *anything*. But I didn't want to have a knock-down, drag-out fight in the house because I didn't want the kids to hear.

She kept insisting that nothing had happened, but now I knew she was lying.

I had no idea how to fix this mess. The following day, all I could think to do was forbid her to take the kids to my mom's. I thought I could keep Angie and Jerry apart that way.

I felt betrayed. I felt angry. I felt as if I might explode.

I went to the garage and rummaged around in an old tackle box where I'd once stashed a bottle of Xanax. There were eight pills left, and I was grateful to find them. That night, I took one, thinking I still had a week's supply. I slept in the guest room.

The next morning, I realized that I'd slept more soundly than I had in years. I felt energized and calm at the same time, as if nothing could upset me, not even Angie.

Angie acted full of remorse, apologizing for being at the motel with Jerry and making excuses about stress and work. She swore that she did not have sex with my brother, but I no longer believed her.

I looked at our two kids and was overwhelmed by the beauty of their innocence. As much as I hated facing the truth about my wife, I couldn't imagine breaking up our family.

I believed in marriage. I believed in God. And I believed that our children should have two parents.

Angie tried to act as though she was truly sorry. She stepped up her game of acting like an adoring wife. She waited on me hand and foot, just like she did when we first met. She kept the house spotless, cooked nice meals, and showed affection toward the kids. But I knew it was false. My life was unravelling.

CHAPTER 11
BAD DECISIONS

AT WORK, the Saturday before Thanksgiving, a woman I hadn't seen in weeks approached me.

"How have you been, Steve?" she asked. "I haven't seen you in awhile."

"Having trouble at home, and I've been trying to get everything done here as quickly as I can so I can get home to the kids."

"I've been there," she said. "My doctor prescribed Xanax for me when I found my husband cheating on me."

"Yeah, Xanax can help," I said. "But I only have two left."

"I can only take a half a dose because they knock me out."

"But I bet you feel better when you wake up. I know I do."

Before I left for the day, that woman handed me six blue tablets, some of her Xanax. "I'm sorry you're going through a tough time. I hope these will help."

On my way home from work, I saw an old, sky blue GMC pickup that looked a lot like my brother's, speeding out of my neighborhood. As I pulled into the driveway, Angie was waiting for me with a big smile. She hugged me and said, "How was work today, honey?"

I smelled alcohol on her breath. "Where are the kids?" I asked.

"They're in their rooms watching TV."

"Why are *you* in such a good mood?"

"Because I just am," she said sloppily.

"Did it ever occur to you that drinking while watching two young children isn't a real good idea?"

She stumbled against the kitchen cabinet, righted herself, and said, "What do you mean? Are you going to ruin my day with your accusations again? I haven't been drinking. "

"Was my brother here today?"

"Of course not," she slurred.

"Then why are you drunk?"

"I only had one drink."

"You don't get this drunk from one drink. You lie, just like my brother does, so that answers my question about him being here. And besides, I saw his truck."

She then began to scream. "So what if he was? He's got nothing to do."

"He's got nothing to do because he's a drunk and a drug addict. He's got nothing, and he *is* nothing. And you you're nothing, too. That's why neither of you have anything to do except sneak around getting drunk all day … in MY house!"

Angie then exploded onto me, punching me with straight hard punches while screaming at the top of her lungs, "I hate you, you fuckin' jerk. I hate you."

When I heard her say, "I hate…" I saw and felt the energy of the evil, ugly thing that was within her, and it was all aimed at me. Her squinting eyes, widened nostrils, and clenched teeth made her look like a monster.

"I wish you could see how ugly you are right now." I said. "You're acting just like my brother does when he goes into his crazy fits of rage. You're two peas in a pod."

She then sat down, took a breath, and with a calm and innocent look said, "Let's go out somewhere with the kids," and then turned and walked off to get the kids, as though nothing had just happened.

I was completely stunned, once again, by what just happened and the way she went from completely crazed to immediate calm. She instantly switched into "good wife" mode and went to gather up the kids, asking them if they'd like to go for a ride in the country.

A ride in the country? Was she serious?

All I could do was go take a shower to clear my head. But first, I hid the six blue Xanax in with my remaining two orange tablets. When I got out of the shower, Angie and the kids were ready to go out for a little field trip, acting like a normal, happy little family.

I thought I was going crazy. Reality was shifting back and forth so fast that I could no longer keep up with it. Her Jekyll-and-Hyde personality switched from one extreme to the other so quickly.

I began to seriously consider that she needed psychiatric help.

Jodi and little Steve were both chanting, "We're going out to the country," when Angie's mood switched again, this time to disgust. When I asked what was wrong, she said, "Nothing. Let's go."

We drove about thirty miles into the country, making stops so the kids could see the horses, cows, goats, and geese. They were having a great time. Angie suggested we stop off at a country store to buy some food and drinks for a picnic. I reminded her that we had no money and had been broke for weeks; she shocked me by saying, "Don't worry. I have money."

She hadn't worked in at least a month, and there was no way she could have any money. I had no idea where she could have gotten it and realized I didn't really want to know.

We stopped near a stream for our picnic, and while the kids were looking for rocks and bugs, Angie grew bored. "I take it you're not having as much fun as the kids are," I said.

"I've had enough of this happy family crap. I want to go home."

And we left.

The next morning I woke up in a panic, thinking I was late for work before I realized it was Sunday. I found Angie sitting at the kitchen table with her cell phone and a cup of coffee. She got up, hugged me, and said, "Good morning,

I didn't want to wake you. Do you want coffee?"

It was a brand new day, the sun was shining, and my wife was acting like a normal person. "Sure, I'd love some coffee." Although I knew better than to trust her, I had gotten into the habit of latching onto any normal moment I could find, so I went along with her masquerade. "I'll run out to get something for breakfast. What would you like?"

"Nothing," she said. "I'm trying to lose weight."

"Angie, can we please talk about what's going on?"

"What do you mean? Nothing's going on." She busied herself pouring my coffee. "Everything's fine. You're just imagining things. Can I make you some eggs?"

"When we first moved here, we were best friends. But you're on another planet now," I said. "When I try to talk to you, you scream at me or accuse me of being controlling. I don't even know who you are anymore."

She said, 'What am I doing wrong?"

"You're sleeping with my brother. Why don't you just admit it?"

Angie got out the skillet, ignoring me.

"Not to mention that you've been fired from two jobs and lied to me about both of them. And you drink so much during the day that you can't take care of the kids. This isn't how life is supposed to be."

She turned around and threw the frying pan at the wall, barely missing my head. "Don't you tell me I'm not a good mother!"

"Really? Then why were you practically doing a striptease in front of the baby?"

"I take good care of the kids!"

"Why do you call them brats? Why do you always hang up the phone the minute I walk into the room? And why on earth are you screwing my brother?"

"I swear, there's something wrong with you, Steve. You're paranoid. You're making all this up."

"Angie, you're getting worse every day. I know you can't see it, but something is seriously wrong. You need help. "

"No Steve, *you're* the one who needs help. You're paranoid and controlling. I'm not doing anything wrong. This is all in your head. Everything is fine. You're constantly nitpicking and looking for problems where there are none. Now leave me the fuck alone."

At that moment our son came into the kitchen rubbing his eyes, and wobbled straight to Angie, with his arms out, wanting her to pick him up.

We lowered our voices, and Angie picked him up, hugged him, and made him some breakfast. The perfect mother.

My mom called later that morning, inviting us for lunch, but I said no. "Mom, I don't want any more of Jerry's mess touching my family."

"Your brother swears nothing happened between Angie and him. Please come over. I miss you guys."

"Mom, Jerry's a liar, I don't trust him, and I don't want him around my family."

But she insisted and promised that Jerry would stay in the basement, so I relented and agreed to come by for lunch. We hadn't seen her for several days, and I didn't want the kids to sense that anything was amiss.

The kids were delighted to be at Grandma's, which was essentially their second home. We had a nice meal, until my brother interrupted things.

"Hey, Uncle Jerry!" the kids said as he emerged from the basement.

Jerry staggered into the kitchen and said, "Hey, everybody." He looked directly at Angie, who was staring at him.

He walked over to the stove, complaining, "Is this all I get is leftovers? What am I, a nigger?"

Mom got up, offering to make him some coffee, and as she did, Jerry sat down in her chair and started eating food from her plate. He looked across the table and said to Angie, "Hi, sweetie pie."

She smiled and blushed and that was it. I grabbed him and pulled him out of the chair.

"Okay scumbag, outside."

"Please don't fight, Steven," my mom yelled. "Don't hit him!"

I let go of Jerry and let him fall to the floor in a drunken heap. He was laughing, and Angie was laughing too.

"Angie, get the kids. We're leaving."

Angie gathered the children, and my mother followed us outside apologizing.

As we drove home all I could think about was how horribly wrong everything was. *Why was Jerry still living with Mom? Why did she put up with it? With him? Why was my wife having an affair with my brother right under my nose, and why was I putting up with it?*

I felt like I couldn't think for myself any more. Mom was pressuring me to keep peace because she wanted a united family and wanted her sons to get along. I wanted to honor her wishes, but the thing that made her happy was the same thing that was tearing my family apart.

From the back seat little Steve asked, "What was wrong with Uncle Jerry?"

I looked at Angie and said, "Go ahead and tell him."

She didn't say anything, so I said, "Your uncle is a drunk."

"What's a drunk?"

"A drunk is a stupid person."

My son thought about that for a minute and then said, "Will I be stupid if I drink?"

"You sure will."

"Then I'm never going to drink, Dad."

Jodi sat in the back seat, quietly staring out the window.

—·—

I realized that like my mother, I was willing to put up with anything just to have the semblance of a happy family.

This couldn't continue. We weren't a happy family.

I knew something had to be fixed, but I did not know how to do it.

I felt my best course of action was to stay away from my brother, which meant staying away from Mom's, and I explained to the kids and my mom that we would not be visiting Grandma for awhile.

I tried to understand why Angie acted the way she did. It was as though she enjoyed the chaos, the violence, the anger.

CHAPTER 12
THE BEGINNING OF THE END

MONDAY, THE DAY AFTER the disastrous lunch at my mother's, I walked into my house, and found Angie waiting for me at the kitchen table. The first thing she said was, "Who told you how I lost my job?"

"Are we still stuck on that?" I asked. "Give it up! What are you gonna do, go after the person who told me, and beat them up?"

"I just want to know."

"Get over it. You sit here at home all day, I don't pressure you to get a job, and you have all the time in the world to drink and screw my brother. You have nothing to complain about. But now, it's time to get your ignorant ass out of that chair and come with me to get Chub."

Chub was so happy to see us when we picked him up that it made me forget the problems with my marriage. After the three of us got home, Chub went off to ride his tricycle, pulling a wagonful of bread and cookies to deliver to the neighbors. One neighbor, a 73-year-old woman, commented on his happy nature and said, "Your boy is certainly polite."

I was proud of my boy and especially of his desire to make everybody around him happy.

"Hey, Chub, are you done?" I asked him. "It's time to go get groceries."

"Okay, Dad." He pedalled as fast as he could to get up the driveway and nearly ran over my foot as he pulled his trike in its spot in the garage.

While Chub had made his rounds of our neighborhood, Angie had changed clothes and was now ready to go to the grocery store. I noticed she wasn't wearing her wedding ring. When I asked why, she said her hands were swollen.

I cleaned up, and Angie put Chub in her car. Even before I left the house, I could hear the bass of her car stereo. I walked down the driveway and saw little Steve in his car seat with his hands over his ears. I opened the passenger door, lowered the volume. "Can't you see Chub is covering his ears?" I said to my wife.

She glared at me and said, "Are you going to start trying to control me again?"

"If that's what it takes to make you lower the volume, then I'm going to take control."

She hit the gas before I could even close the passenger door.

When we got to the first stop sign, I reached over and put the car into park, holding the gear shift firmly. "I don't know what you're trying to prove, and I don't care, but you will not drive like this with our son in the car. Do you hear me?"

Angie screamed, "Don't tell me how to drive, you asshole. I'll drive any way I want."

She put the car back in drive and drove only five miles over the speed limit all the way to the store. Everything went fine while we shopped, and when we were through, I said I'd drive home.

"No, you won't. I'll drive. I've got the keys." She made a point of putting the driver's seat all the way back, rolled down the window and stuck her foot out.

At the first stop sign, I reached over and put the car in park. "You've got to be kidding," I said. "You're jeopardizing our safety, driving like this. Chub's freezing in the back seat. Roll up your window!"

"I am never going shopping with you again," she said, and rolled up her window.

We got home and put away the groceries and then I took a quick nap. I

65

woke up to the sound of kids laughing. Angie was making Chub laugh by doing goofy things and keeping Jodi amused as well.

Her behavior, again running from one extreme to the other, was baffling, to say the least.

About a half hour went by when Angie turned to me and said, "Let's take the kids out to dinner."

Jodi jumped up and down, chanting, "ChuckECheese! I want to go to ChuckECheese!"

Steve chimed in, "I wanna go to ChuckECheese, too!"

The kids, overjoyed at the thought of such an outing, ran towards the garage. I looked at Angie and said, "I have twelve dollars. If we're going there we'll need about twenty or thirty more. "

"I don't have any money," Angie said.

"I thought you said you always have money."

She smiled and said, "No I didn't. I never said that."

What was she? A damn psycho?

"Okay, " I said. "Here is the problem, you don't remember what you say from one day to the next. I don't want to play games while the kids are waiting to go out. We need a few more dollars if we're going to ChuckECheese. Do you have any money or don't you?"

"No, I don't."

"Well then, let's count our change." All we found in the coin jar were pennies and nickels.

We ended up taking the kids to Burger King. We got home about seven o'clock, and Steve wanted to ride his bike, but it was too cold so he settled or playing a video game. after the kids were in bed, I tried once more to talk with my wife.

"Why do you act the way you do?" I asked her.

"What did I do wrong, now?"

"Besides sleeping with my brother? Endangering the kids when you drive? Drinking during the day? "

"I didn't fuck your brother."

"Then why did you shave your pussy?"

"It's none of your business. I can do what I want with my body."

"Do you love me and the kids?"

"Of course I do."

"Then why do you call us names?"

"I don't call you names."

I decided to change the subject. "So what do you have planned for tomorrow?"

"Why do you want to know? What do you care what I do tomorrow? Lay off me, you jerk. You're so damn controlling, I can't breathe around you."

"So it's all my fault?"

Suddenly she smiled and said, "I'm going to look for a job tomorrow. I really should contribute more financially. I'm sorry that I've been out of work so long, honey."

Dr. Jekyll and Mr. Hyde again. Angie could switch gears on a dime to get what she wanted. She wanted the questions to end. And it worked. I stopped asking.

—·—

I decided to try my best to make the welfare of my family my first priority. I spoke to Angie in the nicest way I could. She, in turn, was as nice as could be, and showed genuine concern for Steve and Jodi. We were both on our best behavior. Tuesday, when we went to pick up Chub from pre-school in Angie's car, and she drove like a normal person.

He came out to the car holding a coloring book page that said, "J is for Jesus" and he was pretty proud of it. We were too.

We got home and I said, "Let's have some fun, Angie."

"What do you mean?"

"Let's be kids and show our four-year-old little boy how to play like one." I got on my bike and Chub got on his. Angie ran alongside both of us. She started tickling Steve and he laughed so hard he could hardly pedal.

"I love you, Mommy!" he said at the top of his lungs.

Since things seemed to be going so well, I said, "See, we can make this house a home, if you want to."

"What do you want me to do?" she asked.

"Just love us. I know there is love within you, because I saw it just now when you were playing with Steve. But you have to decide if you're in or out of this marriage. You can't have it both ways. You have to promise me that you won't see my brother again."

She agreed. And for the first time in a long, long while, I felt hope.

Back at home, my son was ready to make his deliveries and he hooked his wagon up to his trike. I opened my bread truck and he scrambled up and loaded his arms with donuts and bagels and two loaves of bread. Steve pedalled down the drive, his wagon bouncing behind him and I walked along the other side of the street, allowing him a little freedom and letting him feel responsible for his deliveries.

When his wagon was empty, he headed for home and steered his trike right toward me, pretending he was going to crash into me.

"Hey!" I said. "You almost hit me!"

He just laughed and raced into the garage and parked his toys. We went in and he ran over to his mom to give her a hug, but she pushed him away.

"You're all sweaty. Get away from me."

"Come on, Chub," I said. It was obvious his feelings were hurt. "Let's go watch some cartoons."

After about five minutes, he was still not smiling. But then, one of the characters on the screen got run over. "Boy, I'm glad you didn't run over me with your bike today, because I would have looked like that, a big flat blob."

He laughed then. "I was gonna make you into a mush pie, Dad."

"You better not!" And we laughed together.

It was past my usual nap time and I needed that hour or two of sleep. I'd been up since one a.m. I slipped into my bedroom for a Xanax and Angie saw me.

"What are you doing?"

"I'm taking a Xanax so I can grab a little rest."

"So now you need to take a pill to go to sleep. You sleep and I have to watch the kids?"

"Look, if I don't take this, I only doze for ten or fifteen minutes. This helps me sleep well for an hour or two so then I can deal with everything during the evening."

"Can I have one?" she asked and then snatched two of the blue tablets from my hand.

"Don't take them both, they're too strong for you."

"Dick."

"I'm going to bed."

Before I laid down, I checked on Steve. He was sound asleep in his room. It was about 3:30 and I was asleep within minutes.

CHAPTER 13
THE ANGELS ARE COMING

WHILE I SLEPT, Jodi got home from school. Angie put both kids in the car and took Jodi to a friend's house and then, when she returned to the car, for some reason, she let Steve sit in the front seat instead of his car seat. Not only was he in the front seat, he wasn't buckled and the windows were rolled down. Unrestrained, Steve stood on the passenger seat while his mother drove over to my mom's house hoping to find my brother. Jerry's truck wasn't there, so she left.

She drove another two miles, looking in the mirror to fix her hair. Distracted, she went off the road to the right, swerved left and lost control of the car, rolling it over onto the left side of the road.

The driver of the car travelling behind them said that she saw a little boy jettisoned from the passenger window as the car rolled over and landed on him. That driver happened to be a nurse. She slammed on her brakes and ran to the scene.

Angie, pulling herself out from the wreckage, yelled, "Save him! Save him! My husband will kill me if anything happens to him!"

The nurse called 911.

At approximately 6:10 p.m., Cabarrus County Emergency Medical Services was dispatched to the scene. First responders lifted the car and carefully moved Steve.

Police officers arrived on the scene. Angie was placed in custody for driving under the influence and several other related charges.

When the paramedics arrived, they found my son lying on the ground beside the car.

Paramedics checked for breathing, but found none. Steve's chest was decompressed and his pupils were fixed and un-responsive. They suctioned his mouth and placed an oxygen bag around his mouth and nose, attempting to fill his small lungs. They inserted an endotracheal tube into his throat and listened to his lungs with a stethoscope. They heard very faint sounds of breath.

Placing him on a back board with head blocks on each side of his face they strapped him onto a stretcher and slid him into the ambulance. The door closed and the driver sped toward Northeast Medical Center's Emergency Room, approximately three minutes away.

Another EMT attended to a small cut on Angie's face, and she screamed, "Save the baby! My husband will kill me if anything happens to him!"

I was at home asleep when all this happened.

I woke up to my mother and sister screaming, "Angie had a car accident and the baby is in the hospital!"

I ran to my car with my shoes in my hand. I didn't want to waste time putting them on.

The EMTs had continued CPR during the ride to the hospital. The moment the ambulance arrived, the ER trauma team jumped into action. After the leads to the EMS heart monitor were replaced with leads to the bedside monitor, there were no signs of life. The patient, my son, was "asystole," which meant that his heart was not pumping.

CPR continued as my son was given two more doses of epinephrine, but still there was no response. The surgeon and emergency physician examined my son's lifeless body and decided that it was futile to continue.

When my mom and I arrived at the hospital, we were met by a doctor, a nursing supervisor and the hospital chaplain. I took one look at their faces and knew the news was bad, and when the doctor told me that little Steve was dead, I thought, *This isn't true. They've made a mistake. How could they be so incompetent?*

They led us to one of the exam rooms, and there was my little boy, lying face up with a sheet covering him up to his neck. His face was bruised and swollen, and I heard a scream come from my mouth — "NO!"

I ripped the sheet away and scooped him up, holding his lifeless body as tight as I possibly could. I remember thinking that holding him that way might propel some life back into him, as if my love and my own life force could flow into his body and revive him.

I begged God not to take him. "He is just a little boy. He does not deserve to die. Take me instead." I begged. I wailed.

Slowly, the thought penetrated through the shock that my son was gone.

Still holding him as close to my chest as I could, I begged Steve to forgive me for letting this happen.

"I am so sorry, I am so sorry. I am so sorry, my boy," I cried.

As his father, my job had been to make sure he was safe. He wasn't safe. He was *dead*. I had failed

I had been responsible for him. I had been his hero and his protector, and I had failed.

How could I live with that. *I am so sorry, dear God, I'm so sorry. Please forgive me dear God, he wasn't supposed to die, I am so sorry.*

My mother put her hand on my shoulder, and whispered, "Let him go now, Steven. The baby is gone."

I let him go as gently as I could, but then something burst open inside of me.

I turned to my mother and said, "Where is she? I'm going to kill her. Where is she?"

My mother looked straight at me and said, "From this moment on, every decision you make, I want you to make as if I am standing on your left side, and Jesus Christ is standing on your right. We are both watching you. Do you understand? Do not let go of that image."

Even in the midst of my pain and rage, I understood, and I agreed.

But I looked at Steve's lifeless body and knew that I would never see him alive again.

I ended up handcuffed, shackled and taken to Broughton Psychiatric Hospital, where I was committed for making homicidal and suicidal threats.

I had gone crazy in the hospital, alternating between screaming, "Where is that bitch? I'm going to kill her," and falling to my knees, crying and begging God to take me instead.

I do remember telling men in white coats, "I know my son is dead, my wife is in jail, and I don't even know where my daughter is, so I need to get home because my family needs me. I don't belong here. I have to leave right now."

The supervisor came in at seven o'clock the next morning and said that I could be released into my mom's care. When I got home, the house was filled with social service people investigating whether our house was a safe environment for Jodi.

I could not deal with any of it. I went straight into a bedroom, where I cried and wailed without reservation.

Being handcuffed and shackled had done something to me. Begging God with everything in me to fix this horror, while holding my son's lifeless body, I had focused all of my energy on trying to get him back. Panic and disbelief in my faith, God, my life, consumed me. When an unemotional police officer restrained me, a cloud of confusion settled over me, leaving me completely lost. I still had a sense of knowing right from wrong, but a line had been drawn — a line between the law and basic morals. The scales were out of balance. I was out of balance.

Exhausted physically, mentally, and spiritually, I cried with such ferocity that I felt my body physically diminish. And I cried even more, with everything I could, hoping to exhaust whatever life-giving energy I had in a vain attempt to make myself die so I could see my son again.

— · —

The next day was Wednesday, the day before Thanksgiving, and my day off. I woke up in a daze. I knew what had happened, but I still didn't want to believe it. I got out of bed and fell to the ground. My legs were numb. I lay on the floor, thinking that I couldn't walk, but that I didn't care, because I was too overwhelmed with grief. I just stayed there crying for my little boy, who had been the life of this house, the life of *me*.

Eventually, I made it to the kitchen, where my mother greeted me. It didn't even occur to me to think about how painful this must be for *her*, and also for Jodi. I hadn't given a thought to either of them; my mind was filled with my own pain — and wrath toward Angie.

Angie was still in jail and my mother said that we needed to discuss funeral arrangements. I asked her to take care of them. I didn't know what to do, and wouldn't have been capable of doing anything even if I'd wanted to.

Mom gave me some coffee and something to eat, which I ignored. Instead, I grabbed my keys and headed out to my truck. I wanted to inspect the accident site.

I got there and tried to visualize and experience what went on during those horror-filled moments. I walked around, not knowing what I was looking for, and then I saw one of Chub's shoes about three feet past where the skid marks started. I picked up the shoe, and sobbed. *This is not real. None of this can be real.*

I saw skid marks that began on the shoulder of the road. I examined every inch of this stretch of road. Embedded in the asphalt I found what I thought was a piece of my son's skin, just a little patch, about the size of a dime.

A lightning bolt of horror shot through my body, and silent thunder boomed in my head, punishing me and tormenting me as I gazed at the proof of his death.

I crossed the road where the bushes were completely crushed by Angie's car as it flipped over. I can almost hear her car stereo blasting.

On my hands and knees, I examined everything. I scanned every grain of soil and blade of grass. I found a four-inch deep impression in the dirt where his body had landed, and in it I discovered a piece of his hair. I held it as gently as I could, because it was a piece of Steve.

Above the impression I noticed a small branch, broken and pointing downward. I lifted the branch and saw a dark stain. It was his blood.

I knelt there, oblivious, until my knees hurt, my back ached. Finally, I stood and staggered back to my truck, driving back to my mom's house in a stupor.

Back at my mom's my brother showed me that my wife had made the front page of the *Independent Tribune*. The headline read "Mom Charged in Child's Death." She was on television, too. I had to deal with the death of my son while acknowledging that my wife was not only an adulterer, but also a criminal. A child-killer.

Mom asked, "What about Jodi?"

I didn't know; I didn't even know where she was. I had literally forgotten about her. I didn't know what was happening.

A woman had called the house, explaining that Angie had dropped Jodi off at her house just before the accident.

Jodi had been there for two days. Did she know what had happened? Who would tell her? Who could explain this nightmare to a young girl when I could barely comprehend it myself.

My brother Jerry went with me to get Jodi. When we got to the house where she had been staying, a man answered the door. He did not want to give Jodi to me until he could see where I lived. This irritated Jerry, and he was about to act out in his usual stupid way, but I said it would be okay. The man followed us home and inspected my house. I assumed that he imagined that Jodi lived in a dump with horrible parents, but I guess he was satisfied with what he saw, and he let her stay with me.

Nonetheless, he called Social Services, expressing concern. He and his wife reported that when Angie had dropped off Jodi she'd told them, "No one is to get Jodi, not even her father."

I couldn't imagine why Angie would have said something like that, but at this point, all I wanted was to have Jodi safe at home with me.

—·—

When Angie called my mom from jail she asked, "How is Chub?"

Mom was stunned. "Angie," she said, "the baby is with God."

Angie paused and then talked about being in jail. After a while she asked again, "How is Chub?"

"Angie, I told you. The baby is with God."

"What do you mean? How is he?"

"Angie, the baby is dead."

Angie's only response was to say that she'd call back tomorrow.

Mom said to me later, "Angie didn't even know that the baby died. Is it possible that they didn't tell her? I don't know if I should be mad at her, or pity her."

"Let's not let anything interrupt our grief right now, Mom. Let's just feel sorry for her." I remembered the beautiful moments I'd witnessed between Angie and Chub during the times when she was in "good mother" mode. Maybe in her way, she had really loved him. Knowing that she was responsible for her son's death must hurt in a way that I couldn't understand.

The next day Angie called complaining that there was no heat in her cell. She was freezing. Can you please bail me out?"

I told her she'd have to wait until Monday when I could get to the bank. "I'll call and see what the problem is with the heat."

"No," she said. "Don't do that. Just get me out."

When I called the jail, they said there was no problem with the heat in their facility.

Mom asked the police if Angie could go to the funeral home to view Steve's body. We still weren't sure that she even knew or understood that he was dead. They agreed, and made arrangements to take her there after hours to protect her from anyone, including me, who was angry over what she'd done. Friday, the day after Thanksgiving, three days after the accident, four armed officers escorted Angie to the funeral home under the cover of dark.

—·—

I worked Friday, but hurried home and picked up Jodi. We ate a quick dinner and went straight to the funeral home.

Walking through the door, I could feel what little energy I had left dissipate.

I had difficulty comprehending anything that was happening that day. I dropped to my knees next to my son's casket and rubbed my face against his; his once warm and rosy cheek felt cold.

I put my hand over the scratch on his face. "I'm so sorry Chub, please forgive me. I'm so sorry I let you down. I am so sorry. Dear God I am so sorry." I begged his forgiveness, for failing as his father, and most of all, for my inability to help him now.

When people arrived to pay their respects, I sensed that something catastrophic was going to happen. As friends and neighbors poured into the room, that feeling grew. When Angie's K-Stores supervisor, Morry, walked in with his wife, I knew. He was the guy who had come to my house in his softball shorts and had run off the moment he saw me.

And there was another guy with him who also worked at K-Stores, someone who used to glare at me every time I went in the store. I knew in my gut that Angie had slept with both of these guys, and couldn't believe they had come to my son's funeral. Morry and his wife went to the casket, and then a moment later he approached me with a smile and asked, "Where's Angie?"

Something exploded inside of me, screaming, *Kill him*. This was my son's funeral and this man doesn't say a word to me, just asks for my wife.

KILL HIM.

But how? Where? Here? Now? How do I kill him without dishonoring my little boy?

KILL HIM.

I looked him straight in the face, took one step forward, and asked, "Do I know you? I don't believe we've met."

Instead of answering, he turned and walked away, confirming everything I'd suspected. He'd slept with my wife.

KILL HIM.

My mind had traveled to a new and different place. My grief had found a new home: vengeance.

I knew this man wasn't responsible for Chub's death, but he was responsible – along with God knows how many other men – for Angie's neglect of her children, her family, *me*.

While I pondered the balance between wanting to kill him and doing the "right thing," The other man asked, "Where's Angie ?"

"In jail."

I pushed past them and went straight to my boy and dropped to my knees. I apologized to God, and my son, for what I was about to do. I was really, truly, literally thinking about how I could kill that man, because I was certifiably insane at this point.

As if the death of my son at Angie's hands wasn't enough, two of her boyfriends came to my son's funeral... asking for her!

I wanted one or both of those men dead, but thankfully, there was still a shred of humanity left in me, and I knew that it would be a mistake to kill them. My anger was off the charts, and in the months and years to come I fought constantly to suppress it.

The funeral took place on Saturday. Angie, still in jail, could not be there to say goodbye to our son.

I did not know how to act at the funeral. Should I say hello to everyone and thank them for coming, as if we were at a cocktail party? Should I be strong and dignified, smiling and greeting everyone like a host? Or, should I let this painful affair take its course without me, staying apart, drowning in my sorrow, disbelief, and guilt?

I did nothing. Just stood there thinking about killing the K-Stores guy.

I stared at Chub's casket, his body. I could hear his voice and smell his scent, but could not feel the power of his life. I kept wondering when this mistake would be corrected, still waiting for death to recognize its error, wake

Chub up, and put him back where he belonged. Time seemed to be running out, as if there was some sort of deadline looming. As the priest conducted the funeral, every word of every prayer was sand pouring down through an hourglass. Time was running out. I started to panic.

The priest said, "Dear God please take Little Steven into your kingdom."

Was something supposed to happen now? What was I supposed to do? Something was happening and I was ready to do something, but I didn't know what it was.

The wind started to blow, and the tent we were sitting under seemed as though it was going to blow away. The priest's Bible was almost blown from his hands, the pages nearly ripped from the binding.

I heard a woman two rows behind me say, "The angels are coming."

I turned to look at her. I had never seen her before. She was about 60 years old, slim and plain looking, with short gray hair and sparkling eyes. In the midst of all the pain around us, she was smiling. Was she a co-worker of Angie's? A member of our church?

The reality of my son being gone hit me the hardest and I entered a place of calmness. All was quiet as the mass ended and everyone walked toward their cars.

I walked past the casket, to see my little boy for the last time. As the men prepared to lower him into his grave, I said, "This is *my* job."

One of the men took a step back and allowed me to help lower my son's casket into the earth. I lowered it as gently as I could so as not to hurt him.

CHAPTER 14
SEEKING JUSTICE, MY WAY

I BAILED ANGIE OUT of jail. Why? I don't know. Nobody could understand why I did it. The short version is she was my wife, and due to my ethics and religious values, I couldn't completely turn my back on her. I drew $2000 from the bank and paid it to the bail bondsman.

As we drove to Mom's after she was released, I asked, "What happened?"

"I do not know," she said.

I asked a lot of questions pertaining to the accident. Her answer to every one was, "I don't know."

At my mother's house, Angie ate lunch as though nothing had happened. Even though our situation was impossibly tragic, some part of me still wanted my family to be intact. I wanted us to work through this together, like a normal couple, with the help of my mom, my brother, my sister and Jodi. Like a normal family. It was a fantasy, but I clung desperately to anything that might make life seem normal again.

Before we'd finished lunch, Jerry came up from the basement. "How you doin', kid?" he asked Angie. He sat down, sharing with us his paranoia about how police and lawyers are the enemy, out to control us and take our money. "The law is out to get you Angie. And since this is such a high profile case, every corrupt lawyer is going to be sniffing around."

Thankfully, Angie said nothing.

After lunch I took Angie to the cemetery to visit our son's grave. In the car, I tried my best to be calm, but just sitting next to her made my skin crawl, and driving in silence made it even more uncomfortable.

Out of habit, I started asking her *why*, just like I'd asked a thousand times before. Why did she drink and drive with the baby in the car? Why didn't she put him in the car seat? Why was she speeding? Why did she sleep with my brother? Why?

She just stared out the window and said, "I don't know."

I could no longer remain calm.

"You were drinking rum and Coke!" I yelled. "Rum and coke is how my brother started and ended all of his relationships, and now you *are* one of those relationships. All of his girlfriends became stupid drunks, and now you're one of them. He beat them all, but instead of getting beaten, you went out and killed our child! You waited for me to go to sleep so you could sneak out of the house. You knew I wouldn't let you drink and drive. What the hell made you do it?"

And again all she said was, "I don't know."

When we got to the cemetery, I fell to my knees at Chub's grave, just a few steps away from my own father's. Sobbing, I told them both how sorry I was. I was vaguely aware of Angie standing next to me.

I should have been there. I should have stopped her. Please forgive me, Chub. I am so sorry, please forgive me, dear God.

I don't know how many times I said these words, and I don't know how long I was there, but I was finally exhausted and knew it was time to leave. I looked over at the truck and there Angie waited in the passenger seat, ready to go home.

I staggered to the truck, got in, looked at her. She had not shed one tear.

"Don't you cry?" I asked. "Don't you have any feelings for that child? Don't you understand what you have done?"

She looked at me. "I know," she said. "He's gone."

I screamed, *"He's gone?* Is that all you have to say? *You killed him.* All that little boy wanted to do was to love you, and now, his dreams, his life, the gifts he brought us, are all gone. You took his life. Don't you feel anything? He was my son!"

"He was my son, too!"

"Then *why, why, why* didn't you put him in the child seat? Why didn't you at least put a seat belt on him?"

"I don't know. I don't know. Please stop it, Steve. Please stop accusing me. This is what you always do; you are constantly accusing me."

I couldn't believe what I was hearing. She was turning this around as if I was doing something wrong. Her reaction seemed bizarre, not only because she didn't seem to have any emotions at all, but because she had no remorse, no sense of responsibility, regret or shame. None.

On the way back to Mom's, driving in silence, some part of me still hoped that Angie would magically transform into a normal person and a good wife. I wanted her to share in my pain. I wanted us to grieve together.

That's why I had bailed her out of jail. I wanted things to feel normal in some way. I had the foolish expectation that she and I could work through this terrible experience together, and that somehow she would be changed by all this, moved by guilt or shame or grief to look at herself, get some help, and *change.*

I was wrong.

Social services returned to ensure that our house was safe for Jodi. They searched everything, asked all sorts of questions, gave us rules and talked to us about the consequences of alcohol and violence in our home.

We passed the safety and livability test.

An insurance agent also paid us a visit. Mom answered the door and he offered her a check for $4000, saying that covered the car, Angie's car that she had totaled. Mom refused the check, told him to leave and never come back. Then she told me to find my insurance policy.

Sure enough, my policy included full coverage on the car, plus a death benefit of $50,000. Without my mom's involvement, I would have just accepted the four grand and been done with it.

Work was no longer a job, it was a penance. The job I once loved and enjoyed was now an exhausting struggle. I cried between stops, and I struggled to talk to my co-workers. I sensed that many of them were afraid to talk to me.

I never realized that a grieving person had the added burden of having to worry about others' discomfort.

On my way home one day, I stopped at the convenience store two blocks from my house to get gas. The clerk said she'd seen Angie waiting in the parking lot for about ten minutes, then saw her get into a white Ford Escort with a man.

Once home, I asked Angie how she'd spent her day. She told me she stayed in the house all day and cried over Chub.

"Someone said they saw you getting into a white car," I told her.

"I went to the store to get cigarettes and asked this lady to give me a ride to the cemetery."

"How come it doesn't look like you've been crying?"

"What am I supposed to look like?" she yelled at me.

I backed off from asking any more questions. Even though I knew the person she'd gotten into the car with was a man and not some lady, I also knew that it was pointless to argue with her.

—·—

Christmas came and went. We did the best we could. Gifts had been purchased that couldn't be given. I thought of Steve's little wish list and broke down. He had just wanted a horn for his tricycle. A tricycle that would never be ridden again.

Looking back now, it must have been hardest on Jodi. I'm sure my mom, who thank God had handled so much of the tragic aftermath of Steve's death, tried to bring a little cheer to Jodi during the holidays. For me, the holidays, Christmas, New Year's, celebrating anything, made no sense at all.

Working out became an obsession, just like going to the cemetery. I didn't know what else to do with my time, my pain, my body or my mind, so I spent an hour each day on the weight machine. Soon I was able to lift twice my body weight, and I got so big that none of my clothes fit anymore. One of the guys at work said I should try out for the Carolina Panthers. I did these workouts religiously, as if I were training for something; as if something huge was going to happen, and I therefore I needed to be in "fighting shape."

—·—

Days when I was able to think clearly, I worried about Angie's future. The charges against her were speeding (60 mph in 45 mph zone), child not in a car seat, D.U.I. (.12 blood alcohol) and felony death by motor vehicle. She faced ten years in jail.

I understood the seriousness of the charges, and realized she had broken the law, but in my crazed state of mind, I believed jail time would not be as effective a punishment as the time Angie could be spending at the cemetery paying her respects to our son. It just didn't make sense that she should sit in jail, where she could ignore her memories of little Steve and the lives she had ruined. It seemed more suitable for her to face up to what she did by coming to the cemetery every day so she could look her crime straight in the eye.

About two weeks after her arrest, I spoke to the district attorney. I wanted to keep my family together, and Jodi needed her mother.

Rosanne Vanderbilt, the district attorney assigned to my wife's case, was adamant about Angie paying for her crime. I pleaded for Angie to be set free, because the respect of my son was more important to me then to have Angie sit in jail, and the only place to pay that respect to him, I felt, was at the cemetery.

Ms. Vanderbilt agreed to reduce the sentence request to 44 months, but I continued to plead and argue until I wore her down and she came up with an offer of 18 months.

I rejected that offer too, and finally, after much pleading and pressuring, Ms. Vanderbilt, perhaps feeling some of the sorrow I was feeling, changed the request to eight days in jail and three years of probation. She also advised me to seek professional help for the trauma I had experienced.

That night I couldn't sleep. I felt as though I'd cheated the law.

The next day I returned to the courthouse, and asked that in the interest of the community, Angie be given 28 days instead.

Ms. Vanderbilt was surprised, but agreed. She also agreed to send Angie to Maryland, where she would live with her sister and do four months of community service while on probation.

At Angie's trial, the judge stated that the sentence was reduced "at the request of the family."

After the trial, Angie and I both went to the cemetery. All I could give my son now were my tears, which I let fall where I thought his face might be, six feet below where we stood.

This had become my ritual; this was the time I looked forward to every day. I would lose track of time and come close to feeling as if I might pass out, and that's how I knew it was time to leave for the day.

And always, after struggling to stand, I'd return to the truck where Angie would be sitting in the passenger seat, impatient to leave.

— · —

On April 5th, 2003 Angie went to jail. She called every other day to talk to Jodi and to me. We tried to support her during this painful and humiliating time, and I did my best to assure Jodi that her mother was safe in jail. We planned to visit her every Sunday.

As a result of her mother's recklessness and the loss of her brother, Jodi began to show signs of bitterness. She said she was embarrassed by what her mother had done.

I suggested that she try to think about all the good times we had with Chub.

She looked at me and started to cry, saying, "Those are the times that hurt the most Dad."

Her teachers sent her to the school counselor.

I came from the kind of family where we took care of our own. Many people offered to help, volunteering to help Mom with cooking and housework while we were in shock, immediately after the accident. She declined those offers, preferring to "keep it in the family."

I didn't seek any help because basically I didn't trust anyone. I felt there was no truth to be found anywhere. I know now that my behavior then was toxic and misguided. I was delusional, still asking God every day to bring my son back. I believed that if I prayed hard enough my prayers would be answered.

On the first Sunday of Angie's incarceration, Jodi and I went to visit. We told Angie that we loved her and missed her, and she seemed happy to see us.

Jodi talked about school and said life wasn't the same without Chub.

We talked about my work and I said it was still difficult.

Angie said she needed $20 for the canteen.

— · —

Jodi and I went to the cemetery every day after school. Afterwards, I would take her to the park to play, as had been our habit before the accident. But it wasn't the same without Chub, and Jodi didn't do much other than walk around staring at the trees and sitting on the bench talking with me.

Life was now so sad. Jodi had lost her joy in life, and seemed more like a shadow of her former self.

Our second Sunday visit to Angie unfolded the same way as the first. Jodi told Angie how she wished we could all be a family again. I told Angie everything was going as well as could be expected while we waited for her to get out of jail.

I gave the guard another $20 for Angie's canteen account, and when I did, I saw in the log book that my brother had deposited $10 on Tuesday. Knowing that my brother was currently unemployed, I figured he had either stolen it or had conned it from my mother.

But how had he managed to visit Angie on Tuesday when visiting hours were only on Sunday?

We lived in a very small town and news traveled fast. As the story about

Chub's death spread, people's responses varied widely, though most had been sympathetic. After Angie went to jail, four different women, in four separate conversations, let me know that my wife had been cheating.

The first woman told me about a guy named Jim Watkins, a stock boy at the BiLo grocery store, who, she said, was a lowlife who tended to complain about everything and still lived with his mother. "He is a piece of garbage," she said and then added, "and so is your wife."

The second woman sounded apologetic, saying, "I'm so sorry that I have to tell you this, because losing your little boy is terrible and I can't imagine what you must be feeling, but this is something you must know. Your wife has had an ongoing affair with a guy named Jim Watkins."

I thanked her.

The third woman approached me in another store and asked if I was the father of the little boy that had died in the recent car accident. When I told her yes she said, "Being that you are the father of that little boy, you should know that I was in BiLo the other day when I heard the stock boys talking. One of them asked, 'How do you feel about your girlfriend now, after she killed her son?' His just said, 'He wasn't *my* son.' This bothered me so much that I had to tell you."

"I've been hearing a lot about this guy at BiLo. I'm sorry this bothered you, but thanks for letting me know."

A fourth woman came to me and told me, "Everyone knew that Jim Watkins had a girlfriend and she was married, because he bragged to everyone that he was dating a married woman. I think this woman was your wife. I didn't know it until now, or I would have told you sooner."

I felt physically ill.

As the stories circulated through our small community, I began to notice that different people reacted to me in different ways. Some kept their distance. Others were kind and compassionate. And although I was on a friendly basis with most of my co-workers, and many of them had heard the story on the news, few had any idea that the woman in the story was my wife.

As people began to put the pieces together and more information came out, some people were angry that I had negotiated a reduced sentence for my wife.

At the same time—I came to learn much later—there were people in town who knew Angie, but did not know me. She had her own circle of friends, and she'd been telling them that I beat her, and molested our children and made her take Xanax on the day of the accident, even knowing that she had been drinking. As these stories circulated around town, I became an outcast.

On top of my grief, I discovered more of Angie's lies and the countless ways she had made a fool of me.

My pain about Angie's behavior got in the way of my pain about my son's death. It was as if Angie was stopping me from grieving. I refused to allow it.

I tried to completely remove Angie from my thinking so I could concentrate on thinking about Chub.

As I did every day, I drove straight to the cemetery after work, and on my hands and knees, told my little boy how sorry I was and how much I missed him. I tried to re-live every moment I could remember. Jodi was so right. It was the good times that hurt the most.

I drove home and waited for Jodi to get home from school. She got off the bus, walking slowly and crying. When she saw me, she ran into my arms sobbing, "I miss Chub, Dad, I miss him so much, I don't know what to do. Everyone looks at me. I hate going to school. I hate everything. I hate Mom. She ruined our lives. She killed my brother. I hate her! She's the worst mother in the world!"

She was shaking and sobbing, and I was crying too, completely at a loss about how to comfort her, how to ease her pain. I had no words to say. I had never dealt with anything like this before.

I had *never* known what to do when bad things happened.

I had always assumed it was best to just let them go. But now seeing Jodi so devastated, I began to feel guilty for letting all this happen. For being so complacent during my years with Angie. Maybe if I'd stood up to her, been more forceful, more angry, or maybe if I had just left her as soon as I found out she was having an affair with my brother—and probably other guys as well—none of this would have happened and Chub would still be here.

With Jodi still crying, and because I didn't know what to do, I simply distracted her.

"Hey, let's go see Grandma. Put your books in the truck, and I'll help you with your homework when we get there. But first let's wash our faces; we both look a little rough."

"Okay, Dad. Can we take the dog?"

"Of course." Chelsea had been neglected since Chub's death. She spent most of her time just lying around whimpering. I imagined she was grieving too and I was happy to take her on a little outing.

So off we went to seek Mom's wisdom.

Mom was surprised to hear about Jim Watkins, and then, in the middle of our conversation, as if on cue, the basement door swung open and my brother burst into the kitchen. He'd overheard us talking, and was furious to learn that she'd been cheating on *him*.

"She's a fuckin' whore!" he screamed, as he stormed out of the house.

It seemed odd that he was more upset than I was, and he had no qualms about letting everybody know. He'd been having an affair with *my* wife, but was furious to learn that she was sleeping with other guys as well. What did he expect from her? Fidelity?

Of course, I was just as blind to her behavior as my brother had been. I was thinking that he had no right to expect anything better from her, and realized that I should have been saying the same thing to myself all this time. I had not been honest with myself about my wife, and now, seeing Jerry's reaction, a light bulb went off in my head that seemed to snap me out of a fog.

I'd been so busy trying to hold my little family together that I'd willingly looked the other way every time Angie had done something awful. And now, in the midst of the worst possible heartache and grief over losing my little boy, I realized I was still habitually making excuses for her. As much of a loser as Jerry was, his reaction to being cheated on was a lot healthier than mine.

Mom said, "I feel as though I was part of the problem, too. I never questioned why Angie left the kids here every day when she was unemployed and had nothing else to do. She must have left them here so she could be with her other men. I'm sorry, Steve. I loved the kids so much that I couldn't get enough of them, so I never questioned her. I was always so happy to be with them."

"It's not your fault, Mom," I said, feeling as if I had finally arrived at the truth. "Angie has a way of manipulating people and pulling them into her web. It's like she casts a spell so that nobody around her can think clearly." I told her that there had been times, when faced with the crazy, dangerous things Angie did, I had been completely paralyzed. "Mom, it was like my brain went to sleep and I couldn't react like a normal person."

This revelation stunned me. It was as if I'd been walking around with my eyes out of focus and suddenly I was able to see the things clearly. I had to face the fact that much of this was *my* fault because I had chosen to ignore everything she did.

I had never put two and two together, but I knew it was time. "She's done enough damage. I have to be done with her once and for all."

But even though I told Mom this, some small part of me still wanted to forgive her and to bring her home from jail to rebuild our life together.

CHAPTER 15
FACING THE TRUTH

ONE DAY, on my way to work, I noticed that I was being followed by a little white car, perhaps a Honda Civic. At the time, I didn't give it much thought.

In one of the stores on my route, while I put bread on the shelves, a couple at the end of the aisle stared at me. I ignored them and continued to work. At my next stop I checked in with Judy, the store manager. She and I had met at another job three years earlier. Normally, we talked and joked together, but today she acted cold. On my hands and knees, putting bread on the bottom shelf, knowing that I was alone there, I allowed the tears to fall. A minute or two went by and I heard someone whisper my name.

I looked up, and there was Judy, crying. I felt terrible, thinking she was crying because she felt sorry for me, and I apologized for making her cry.

She said, "Steve I'm so sorry but I have to tell you this, I just found out that your wife has been cheating on you."

I couldn't believe I was hearing this again. I looked at her and simply said, "I know."

With tears in her eyes and a look of disbelief, she asked, "Then why did you plead for her to get out of jail?"

I replied with my stock answer, which by now was beginning to sound ridiculous. "I just found out about her cheating myself. But she is still my son's mother. What else could I do?"

Judy said, "I lost my daughter when she was a baby, 16 years ago, and the pain was dreadful. I see and feel what you're going through over little Steve, and I know how much you loved Angie. But how are you handling this? Are you getting any kind of help?"

"There is no help. Nobody can help with this. And truthfully, I don't know what I'm doing. I do my job every day because I have to. It's just a reflex, and I can't wait to finish my job so I can go to the cemetery."

She said, "I understand that. I really do. But how can you bear Angie still being part of your life after everything she's put you through?"

"I don't know. I don't know anything. It's too much to think about."

Back in my truck I wondered how Judy had heard about Angie cheating. I figured the whole town must know.

I got to my last stop, and as I walked into the store, the vendors and employees became quiet. It was strange. *What was going on?* I felt as if something else – something new – had happened, and everybody knew about it but me.

No one seemed to talk to me the way they once had. I'd walk into stores and feel everyone's eyes on me. *Do they all know about Angie's affairs?* I wondered. *Do they sympathize with me, or do they judge me for being so blind? What else do they know about her that I don't know?*

I was confused, alone, and afraid. But of what? What was happening?

—.—

The days and weeks dragged on, and I still did my job, but between stops, alone in my truck, sometimes I was consumed with grief and cried uncontrollably.

I wondered where my son was. My faith told me that he was in Heaven, which I honestly and truly believed, but I didn't really know what Heaven was. Trying to picture Heaven did me no good, because the bottom line was, he wasn't with me.

I vaguely remember a buddy of mine – a guy who delivered Budweiser – asking if I was okay while we were both unloading our trucks at a BiLo grocery store. I could hear what he said, but I could not understand what he meant. I remember assuring him that I was fine as I continued to unload bread, but I knew as soon as I said it, it wasn't true.

I was *not* fine. I could still do my job, but I was losing my grip on reality.

Then I heard the same words again, "Steve, are you all right?"

This time it was Kate asking, one of the women who had first told me about Angie's affairs. While the sounds all around me blurred, I could hear her voice with crystal clarity. I saw the sorrow in her face, I felt her kindness, and told her that I was okay but struggling. She handed me her telephone number and said, "If you need anyone to talk to, call me, I'm a good listener."

I was very grateful for someone to talk to, and she was a good choice. I could actually hear and understand what she was saying to me better than I could understand anyone else. Kate showed a genuine concern for my well-being, and I really did need someone to talk to.

At BiLo one day, while Angie was still in jail, Kate mentioned that my brother had been in the store asking about Jim Watkins.

"Are you sure it was my brother?"

"He's a bigger version of you, and he had a Yankee accent. He was asking for Jim Watkins. The whole store knows what happened, and now people are really worried. Be careful, Steve, because Jim Watkins has a lot of kin."

I got in my truck and headed toward my next stop. Four guys in a red Daytona Charger followed me. As I pulled into the Food Lion parking lot, the truck continued down the road. I parked my truck on the side of the store and made my delivery.

When I returned to my truck, the Charger was parked about ten car lengths away, and four guys sat there staring at me. The one in the passenger seat did all the talking. He had a stupid, goofy look about him, and wore big, thick-framed glasses. It was Jim Watkins, and he'd gathered up some friends to protect him while he taunted me about his affair with my wife.

— · —

The next Sunday during our weekly visit with Angie, Jodi acted very cold towards her mother. I told Angie that when she got out of jail we would need to have a serious talk.

"Talk about what?" she asked.

"We'll talk about it when you get out."

But then Jodi said, "Dad *knows*, Mom."

"Knows about what?"

"He knows about you and Jim Watkins!" Jodi screamed. "The whole town knows!"

Angie, in her best fake-innocence voice, asked, "Who's Jim Watkins? What are you two talking about? Don't I have enough to deal with? I'm in jail for shit's sake. Are you accusing me of cheating on you again?"

It was the same tone she had used when I asked her if she noticed the guy starting at us at McDonald's in Myrtle Beach. Another Oscar-winning performance.

I stared at her, watching to see if there was any twitching of her skin or mouth, and listened for any waver in her voice. There was none. She was able to lie so convincingly that I am certain she believed her own lies.

I had never really taken the time to study her this way. Boy, she was good, really good—or should I say really *bad*. She had tricked me for years, but I wasn't blind anymore. Now I simply wondered how she developed this uncanny ability to deceive.

Was it a genetic trait inherited from her mother Edith, who obviously had raised a brood of deranged offspring? I was now more convinced than ever that Angie's sister Dorothy had killed her brother. And then there was the other brother, the one who had practically gnawed off his arm trying to escape from their attic. What kind of family did Angie come from? What kind of horrors had she experienced in her childhood to turn her into such a monster?

Jodi and I left the jail not saying a word. When we got into the truck Jodi broke down. "I can't believe she would lie to us like that."

All I could say was, "There's a lot about your mom that we don't know. It seems there's something new every day. I'm so sorry, Jodi. I'm so sorry for not realizing it sooner. Please forgive me."

On May 3rd I got a call from the Cabarrus County Jail. It was Angie. Apparently she had finished serving her time. She said she wanted to come home and rebuild our life.

"No way. You cheated on me and the kids and killed our son. Go to your boyfriend's house. You have no more home here."

And I hung up the phone.

I did not want to see her. There was nothing left in her that was good. She was pure evil. She could lie and steal with no shame. She had proven to be a pathetic whore who had killed her own son.

A moment later the County Sheriff's Office called again. The clerk there reminded me that the judge's order required Angie to be released to her own home. She would now be under supervised probation and had to be at that address.

"No way," I said again. "Tell her to call one of her boyfriends, and let her stay with one of them."

This was not my usual way of dealing with things, and it scared me. But it felt good at the same time. I was standing up for myself—against the law—because it felt like the morally right thing to do.

Except, I went up against the law by refusing to do what I had agreed to do just months ago, by court order.

I had been the one who had pleaded for her to come home rather than go to jail.

At Mom's, a little later, I told her what I'd done.

"Good," she said. "You did the right thing not taking her back. You can't have a life with someone like her. Do you remember the day she was leaning against this wall and said, 'I've got it made?'"

I did remember that day. We were picking up the kids, and she leaned against the wall just smiling saying how great life was with someone to care for her kids and someone else to take care of everything else. "I don't even have to lift a finger," she'd said smiling.

"That shows how selfish and truly sick she is," my mom said. "It shows how deceived we all were. It's a sin to use your family for your evil deeds, but it's a sacrilege to look them in the eyes and smile while you know that what you're doing is hurting them. Stay away from her," Mom cautioned, "but if she comes around, whatever you do, don't hit her."

"I won't hit her, Mom. I'm afraid that if I did I'd punch a hole right through her. This is above me. This is above the law. Only the Lord can handle her now."

And as I said that, I lost that nervous knot in my stomach and forgot all about her for the time being.

— · —

A few weeks later, I heard that Angie was out of jail. Apparently the court had found a way to work around the requirement that she come back to my house. One of the women who worked at BiLo said Angie had moved in with Jim Watkins.

"Good, he can have her, because I'm done with her. They're both pathetic." It felt good to have such a firm conviction about this. I said it, and I meant it.

The woman said, "But she's still your wife."

"Oh no she isn't. She broke that bond a long time ago, and I've earned my freedom from her. I don't know where she is, and I don't want to know."

But in truth, it was far from finished.

When I heard from another woman at a different store that Angie was staying at the Battered Women's Shelter, I asked "What's she doing there?"

Much as I wanted to be finished with her, I hoped she hadn't been beaten by someone in jail, or become the victim of someone in town acting as a vigilante.

"When you refused to take her back," the woman told me, "she had nowhere to go, so the law put her in the shelter."

"Good," I said. "The shelter is better than where she put my little boy."

CHAPTER 16
SHELTER

DESPITE EVERYTHING, knowing that the woman I was married to, the mother of my child, was living in a Battered Woman's Shelter didn't sit right with me.

I revisited the idea that had formed when I had bargained with the district attorney to reduce Angie's jail sentence. It was the only thing I could think of that might force her to take some responsibility for what she had done. I was determined to *make her see*.

"Look, as long as you're living in this town, I will not let you get away without facing what you've done. I'm going to take you to the cemetery every day to force you to look at that grave."

She said nothing, but nodded in agreement about going to the cemetery with me. And for a few days, I'd stop by at the shelter after work, pick her up, and we'd drive to the cemetery.

She would walk to Chub's grave, make the sign of the cross, and walk back to the truck, leaving me there alone. I spent about five minutes praying, and when I would return to the truck she would be irate. "How dare you make me wait so long!"

I thought the only thing that kept me from killing her and her scumbag boyfriend was the fear of my Lord. I knew that we're not supposed to kill, but even so, there was an unrelenting feeling inside me that wanted to kill her, brutally, like she killed Chub.

And that scared me.

This was partially why I went and prayed over my son's grave every day, because he kept my soul clean. I refused to lose my soul for anyone. Maybe I had already lost it, but now I wanted to take it back.

Each day, as I turned onto the street where the shelter was, I'd tell her that I would pick her up again the next day to take her to the cemetery. For as long as she was in North Carolina, I intended this to be her penance.

This plan of mine didn't go well; I tried to force Angie to take responsibility; I tried and failed. I tried to make her tell the truth.

When confronted by the fact that everyone knew about Jim Watkins, Angie continued to swear she knew no one by that name.

My temper was at the surface, threatening to boil over at every turn.

"You have perfected your craft," I say.

"What craft?"

"The craft of lying, cheating and stealing."

"I don't steal."

"Yes, you do. You stole form your job and lost it. You stole from me and the kids, taking my money to buy my brother clothes, alcohol, and to rent a motel room. You've stolen time away from us, choosing instead to be with two loser boyfriends, forty-year-old men who still live with their mothers. You disgust me. You know the only thing that stops me from killing you?"

"What?"

"Fear of the Lord."

I drove her back to the shelter and as we got close, I noticed none other than Jim Watkins walking toward the shelter. When he saw my truck, he turned quickly in the other direction.

"That's him isn't it?" I asked Angie. "Jim Watkins? The guy everyone in town is talking about? The guy you claim you don't know?"

"I don't know that guy," she said.

I hit the gas and drove past the shelter.

She looked concerned and said, "Where are you taking me?"

"Why do you look so worried? Are you afraid I'm going to take you out into the woods, give you the beating you deserve and leave you there to die? I wish I could, but don't worry, I'm going to do something even worse. I'm going to take you to see your daughter. Have you even thought about her at all lately? Or are you going to abandon her like you did Mary?"

Angie stared straight ahead and said nothing.

Again, I thought if I could just force Angie to see what I saw, the damage that she'd caused, the fact that she still had a daughter who needed her, if I could make her see, she would change.

"You've been out of jail for over a week," I said. "You haven't even called your daughter. I've kept you in my life because Jodi needed a mother and a father. Lately, I've been both to her, but she needs you."

As we entered the house, Angie said she wanted to wait outside by the pool. After a few minutes, I joined her on the deck. I found her naked, lying on the lounge chair with her legs thrown wide. She saw me and said "Fuck me!"

"Not in this lifetime," I said, disgusted."Jodi will be here in a few minutes. Get up and put your clothes on. "

Seconds later Jodi was walking up the driveway.

I said, "Hey, Jodi, I have a surprise for you!" I hoped she might be happy to see her mother.

Jodi walked up to me and whispered, "I love you Dad. I missed you today."

"I love you too, and I missed you. How was school today?" I glanced at the deck and saw Angie run into the house, her clothes in her arms.

"It was okay, Dad. What's the surprise?"

"Come on in the house. "

We walked inside, Jodi telling me about her day. The bathroom door opened and Angie walked out.

Jodi tried to hide her shock, and simply said, "Hi, Mom."

Angie, trying to act like a normal mother, asked, "How was school today?"

Jodi didn't answer. She couldn't even look at her mother.

"What is the matter with you?" Angie asked.

"What's the matter with *me*? What is the matter with *you*? Where have you been?" Jodi shouted. "You've been out of jail for a week and you haven't even called. You don't love me. You suck as a mother. Dad had to drag you over here, didn't he?"

Angie said, "Your dad threw me out so I couldn't come to see you."

Before I had a chance to say anything, Jodi screamed at her mother, "You're lying! And even if that was true, which I know it isn't, why didn't you at least call? You just left me and Dad alone. You're a terrible mother. I hate your guts."

"Don't yell at me, I'm your mother. I gave you life."

Angie's words hung in the air for perhaps ten seconds, and then Jodi started to cry.

I looked at Angie's expressionless face, and said, "I can't believe you said that."

With my surprise backfiring, I told Jodi to go to wash up, and get ready to go out for something to eat. She was happy to oblige.

Although I was disgusted with Angie, the part of me that still naively hoped for something resembling a normal family life was still alive, and there were times when it overrode logic and self-preservation. This was one of those times, because instead of taking Angie straight back to the shelter, I invited her to join Jodi and me for dinner.

During dinner we tried to make small talk, but it was a joke, and afterwards we rode to the shelter in silence, Angie texting on her cell phone the whole time. When Angie got out of the car, Jodi said, "Will I see you tomorrow, Mom?"

Angie said, "I don't think so."

Jodi said, "Why not?

Angie said, "I'll be busy tomorrow. I just can't."

"Haven't you've punished us enough," I asked Angie. "Is this what you feed on? Making everybody around you suffer? You will be ready for me outside the shelter tomorrow at 12 o'clock or *I* will make *you* suffer. You are going to the cemetery with me tomorrow — and every day — to pay respects to our son. I don't care about you, my scumbag brother, your sneaky bastard boyfriend, or whatever immoral shit you're involved in. You will go tomorrow or else. Do you understand me? No more lies, no more cheating, no more disrespectful shit out of you. Do you hear me?"

Jodi had never heard me speak like that before, but just as I was beginning to feel really bad about blowing up like that in front of her, she said, "Hey, Dad, there's Jim Watkins."

Sure enough there he was, with his goofy-looking glasses, walking into the shelter. That's who Angie was texting in the car. He was waiting for her!

That was it. "We're done. Right now," I said. The next day we went to see my lawyer.

After hearing our sorry tale, the attorney looked at us and immediately drew up the divorce papers. Angie and I both signed without a word.

Marriage dissolved.

CHAPTER 17
ANOTHER LOSS

I BECAME OBSESSED with trying to understand how Angie remained so calm and cool while I was an emotional mess. On our trips to the cemetery, I watched her every move trying to understand how the two of us could respond in opposite ways to the same catastrophe. We went through our usual rituals at the cemetery. Her lack of remorse got under my skin.

I had never actually seen her cry. "Don't you ever cry?" I finally asked.

She just looked at me without any expression.

My emotions took over. "Don't you understand that you killed Chub? Don't you understand that you killed our baby?"

She answered me quite calmly, "So? He's dead."

The next thing I knew, her eyes were bulging out of her head with her tongue hanging out of her mouth.

While something inside me screamed, *Kill her*, another voice whispered, *Thou shall not kill*.

I watched her gasp for air, and I didn't care. I was hoping she'd die.

I had really wanted to kill her; I felt as if I was supposed to.

But I couldn't, because it would have been wrong.

And yet, I felt guilty for *not* killing her.

Nothing made sense any more.

I must have been crazy.

The next day two police cars pulled into my driveway and two social service cars parked in front of my house.

I asked the first officer what was going on, and he told me, in a very nice way, almost apologetically, that this was standard procedure in cases like this. They had come for Jodi.

I didn't know what he meant by "cases like this."Another loss. *I am now losing my little girl.*

I assumed Angie called them because I assaulted her, but I don't know for sure. They talked to me, but did not arrest me.

They were very nice, and the officer asked me to stay on the other side of the house while Angie and social services came in to pack up Jodi's things.

After about fifteen minutes, with two women and two police officers flanking Angie and her daughter, Jodi walked up to me, hugged me, and said, "I love you. Dad. I'm gonna miss you."

I hugged her back and said, "I love you, too. I will always love you, and please don't ever forget your brother Chub, because he loved you very much and still does. Please don't ever do what your mother has done. Make me proud of you."

She looked so sad. "I will, Dad," she said.

She got into one of the social services car and they left.

One of the police officers said, "You're a good guy, Steve."

I looked at the officer and said with tears in my eyes, "Thanks. But I guess not good enough."

Despite this, our daily trips to the cemetery continued. A few days later, when I arrived at the shelter, I saw my brother Jerry, waving to me as he came around the corner as if it was the most natural thing in the world for him to be there.

Angie and Jodi got into the truck without saying a word. I asked Jodi how she was and she said, "I'm okay, Dad."

Angie and I didn't say a word to each other.

I tried to stay calm and forget how angry Jerry made me.

At the cemetery, we went through our separate rituals—me lingering at the grave and Angie returning quickly to the truck. Jodi stood with me and put flowers on her little brother's grave.

Afterwards, I suggested that we go back to the house so Jodi could play with Chelsea. Maybe seeing Jodi would cheer up the dog a bit.

Angie agreed, but said, "We can't stay long; I have to be back at the shelter at two o'clock for a meeting."

"A *meeting*? Are you on the board of directors for the shelter now?" I said. "What kind of meeting could you possibly have? Spare me the bullshit, please."

Chelsea greeted us, excited to see her playmate. The two of them went outside and started running around while Angie and I sat at the kitchen table.

"Why was my brother hanging around the shelter?"

"He just wanted to talk."

"He did not just want to talk."

"He doesn't have any friends, Steve. He just wanted to talk." Angie stood and said, "It's time for me to go. I have to go to my meeting."

"What meeting do they have at the shelter at 2:00 o'clock in the afternoon? And since when are you so responsible that you care about getting to a meeting on time?"

"They are going to give us a list of duties and what is expected of us."

"Well it looks as though you are going to be late, because first of all, I don't believe you, and second of all, we'll leave when Jodi is done playing with the dog."

"I have to go right now."

I said, "You'll just have to wait."

At 1:45 we got in the truck and headed toward the shelter, and the whole time Angie yelled at me to go faster. When I got to the corner she said, "Drop us off here."

"Why here?"

"Because it is a Battered Women's Shelter and men aren't allowed on this street."

But I'd seen men there before, specifically Angie's men...my brother and Jim Watkins. Just as she opened the door and got out, a man in a beat-up white car parked in front of the shelter, leaned over the passenger seat calling, "Angie, Angie!"

It was my brother.

Angie did not even look at him as she and Jodi walked into the shelter.

I pulled right next to his car and said, "Looks like I ruined your date with my wife, asshole." And I sped off.

—·—

I was overcome with a giant wave of sorrow, and was more exhausted than I had ever been in my life. I was in a daze, crying and wondering how any of this could have happened.

Most nights I'd lie in Chub's bed thinking about how much I'd lost.

The loss of my son was impossible of me to fathom, and my guilt for being asleep when it happened crushed my soul and dropped me to the floor at least ten times a day. If only I hadn't taken that Xanax.

I'd also lost my wife and all my illusions about marriage and family life.

And on top of that, now I had lost Jodi, the little girl who called me "Dad," who trusted me with her safety and well-being. As a stepfather, I had no legal rights, but she was my daughter just the same.

One night, I heard a loud vehicle on my street. I looked out the window and saw my brother climbing out of an old pickup truck.

I chose to ignore his knock on the door.

But he didn't quit. He started pounding on the door even harder, yelling, "Come on out here you mother fucker I'm going to kick your ass. You fuckin' scumbag, you told Angie I fuck niggers. Come on out here you mother fucker, I'm going to kick your ass."

The phone rang and it was Mom, warning me that Jerry was on his way over in a drunken rage. She begged me not to hurt him.

I looked outside and saw him holding a beer in his hand, peeing in my grass.

I decided to ignore this circus and went back to my son's room.

My wife's boyfriend continued his drunken display of ignorance for a few more minutes, when I guess he got tired and left.

Not much later, the police pulled into my driveway. They said that they were responding to a call regarding a disturbance. I told them that it had been my drunk brother acting like a jerk.

They were as nice as could be and asked if there was anything I wanted to do about him.

I said no, because my brother was just being himself: stupid. Besides, I didn't want any more trouble for my family.

I called Angie. "What did you tell my brother? He's been here, drunk and saying crazy stuff."

The conversation went nowhere, as usual, with me asking questions and her telling lies. All the while I kept asking myself, *Why, why, why do I continue to look for answers with this woman? There ARE no answers, and there never will be. Just give it up!*

But I couldn't give it up.

I decided to tell her about all the gossip I'd been hearing, about all the sex I'd heard she'd had with former bosses and co-workers; strangers, as well. "Remember that tall redneck with the rebel hat? The one you said was just asking for directions to the mall? I hear you did him in the back room of K-Stores, and he got transferred because his wife caught you both."

"Who's saying all of this about me?" she asked. "They're all lying."

"Really? At least a dozen people told me the same story. I guess they're all lying, and you're the only one telling the truth."

She hung up.

— · —

I felt more and more isolated. I no longer had a wife or children. I felt as if everyone at work was avoiding me.

The only consistent human contact I had was with Angie.

I got home from work at noon every day and went straight to get her at the shelter, and every time, I'd find her coming up the street while some guy would be walking down the street in the opposite direction. Some days it was my brother, other days I'd see Jim Watkins, or some other guy hanging around.

I called her every night at around nine p.m., and I'd always hear a beep on the line. I realized later that nine p.m. was the time that Jerry had always called her during our marriage, after the kids and I had gone to bed, and the beep I heard was her call waiting alert, because he was continuing to call her at the same time.

—·—

One day, while delivering bread to BiLo, my friend Kate, the nice woman who had befriended me a while back, approached me in a fury. "What are you saying about me, Steve? Stay away from me or I'll call the police."

I had no idea what on earth she was talking about.

Which was not unusual, because I was so out of touch that I had no idea of what was going on around me most of the time.

I feared the whole town was talking about me, but I had no idea what they were saying.

This upset me because Kate was my friend.

Had I done something that I wasn't aware of? I know I would never do anything to anyone to make them act like this way toward me, but with my state of mind so messed up, it's possible that I might have done terrible things without even being aware of them. What was Kate talking about? I asked her so many times but all she did was scream at me, and I never got an answer.

After work, I went to the cemetery, then went to see my mother. I hoped she could help me figure out what was wrong.

"We can't talk here anymore, Steve," my mom said. "Every time we talk

Jerry listens in and tells Angie."

So we drove over to my house, and I told Mom about how crazy my friend Kate had acted.

She thought it was possible that Jerry, or Jerry and Angie, were behind the gossip and were turning my friends against me.

"Is Jerry really that crazy?" I asked.

"I don't know what's wrong with your brother, and I don't know why he does the things he does, but remember this started with Angie. I'm not saying Jerry is innocent... he's sick, too. But the two of them together are like dynamite, and nobody is safe. She suffers from a sickness that you cannot help, and sadly, Jerry does, too. It is inevitable that they would meet each other, but that doesn't mean you have to let them control your life. Can't you just leave her alone? Why do you have to drag her to the cemetery every day? Do whatever you need to do to take care of your pain, but don't give her another thought. You can't change her, you can't make her feel, and you can't make this right. You just have to learn to accept it the way it is."

"That whore has got to get on her knees and pray."

Then Mom lost her temper. "You can't MAKE a person pray! You can't MAKE anybody do anything, Steve! *You can't change her.* Your only job right now is to heal your own heart. She doesn't matter anymore. It's between her and God, and you can't intervene. You're not God."

But I didn't listen.

I wish I had.

Instead, I went to the shelter and took Angie to the cemetery. She grudgingly went along, stood by the grave for a minute, and went back to the truck.

"I want to go by the house," she said after I started up the truck.

I asked why. She very sweetly said, "I miss it."

I knew something was up because she was acting too nice, but I took her to the house anyway. She walked straight through to the pool, stripped naked and jumped in.

To my astonishment, she swam the length of the 30-foot pool with perfect form, then flipped and swam the length again. When she reached where she started, she flipped over and swam backstroke across the pool. She flipped again, and this time she swam a length underwater, her body undulating like a mermaid. After a couple of laps, she climbed out of the pool, dried off, and gave me a wicked smile.

She had always insisted that she couldn't swim and said she was terrified of the water.

CHAPTER 18
LETTERS

THE MONTHS PASSED, and Angie had nearly completed her community service in Concord. Two weeks before that four-month stint was done, one of Angie's friends from Baltimore drove down to collect the remaining clothes and furniture from Jodi's room. She took Jodi with her to Baltimore. Another chapter of my life had closed.

A few days before Angie herself was to leave for Baltimore to serve her three-year probation, I decided to try one last time to learn the truth about her affairs. Like an idiot, I tried asking her, as if I expected to get an honest answer. The only answer she gave me was, "I never had an affair."

Same shit, different day. But I couldn't leave it like that. So I came up with another ridiculous idea. I asked her to write everything down on paper. In exchange, I agreed to give her an early payment on our divorce settlement.

"I have the money right here," I said, "and here's a pad of paper and a pen on the table. If you want the money, write down an explanation of all the rumors I've heard, all the men I've seen you with. All of it."

I went to take a shower, and when I got out Angie handed me a letter.

8-1-03

Dear Steven,

I am so sorry for cheating on you. I am writing this to you because I owe you the truth. I had an affair that lasted 1 year 6 months with a guy named Jim Watkins. He came to me + we talked and when we had our problems I went to his house because he asked me. We talked + had sex for about 1 year. The last 8 months, I started drinking and I didn't realize how bad I got. I am writing this to you because I would leave his house drinking. I feel that this led to my accident and I am so sorry for the death of Chub. I think about Chub and everything I have done wrong in my life. Also, I am sorry for giving in to James and not trying to work it out with you. Please forgive me for all I have done. This I beg of you.

Love always + so sorry,

A.

    I handed her a check and said, "If this were a fair and just world, I wouldn't have to give you anything. But instead, I have to give you everything I have, including what was left of the insurance money for Chub's death, which amounted to about $25,000. I just hope you'll start your life again in a better way, and get some help for your mental illness... and for Jodi." She wanted her wedding ring back, but I refused to give it to her.

    I looked at the letter again, and while I was re-reading it, she said, "Fuck you and your stupid letter. I only wrote it because you forced me to. I didn't mean a word of it."

    She packed her things, and at one point asked if she could have one of the special paintings I'd had made of Chub. I had two of his photos blown up to life-size and taken them to a painter who enhanced them and made them more life-like. I gave her one, and said, "I did the best I could with this picture, just like I did with our marriage; please don't make a mockery out of this, too."

She tried to hug me, but I would not let her touch me.

As she pulled away, I felt relieved knowing that someone this evil was no longer part of my life. But on the flip side, I was terribly saddened to lose the person who was at one time my best friend, or at least pretended to be. She was the mother of my child—she gave me that wonderful bundle of joy named Chub, and she also took him away.

I moped around the house for several hours and then went to Mom's. She greeted me with hugs and tears, saying, "I'm so sorry for everything that has happened, but most of all, I'm sorry for little Steve. He did not deserve what happened to him, but at the same time I know that he is not really gone. You know you will see him again in Heaven, don't you? Let that bring you comfort instead of always thinking about all the bad things Angie did. Look at the future now. Chub would not want you to be this angry at his mother. He's at home with God now, and he is pure love. Let him teach you how to forgive."

She asked me to stay for dinner but I said, "No thank you, Mom. I think it's best that I never see Jerry again."

"Jerry left this morning," she said. "He's moving in with some girl named Tanya out in Shelby. He met her on the internet."

Wow. Angie had barely crossed the state line, and he was moving in with someone else. So much for his devotion.

"Mom, for nine years he lived in your house without a job, for the last two years he had an affair with my wife and turned her into a sneaky drunk who killed my son. He beats up women and old men, and he's a drug addict. He's not my brother anymore. We're done. And if you consider that piece of shit part of our family, then you and I are done, too."

"Steve," she sobbed, "you are BOTH my sons. Jerry was once a sweet little boy, just like Chub. You know what it's like to love a child like that. Can you see that as Jerry's mother, I love him in a way that only a mother can? Just because he has done you wrong doesn't mean I can turn my back on him. Both of my sons need me."

Damn. She was right. How could I argue with that logic?

Mom hugged me, still crying, and I could sense there was more going on. "What else is going on?"

"As your brother was leaving this morning, he handed me this letter and said that I might need it."

It was a letter to Jerry, in Angie's handwriting.

Jerry,

Hi, I Just wanted to say I am so in love with you. And I want a lot more than you want out of this. I know I was the one that wanted just a kiss. My feelings for you now are stronger than they ever have been before. My thoughts have been of nothing but of you. When I first laid eyes on you, I knew you were made for me. I feel so in Love with you and you make me so Happy when I am with you and when I am not I wish I was. I think about you all of the time. And wish things could be different. And I am not seeing nobody else. When I am with you, you make me feel so good. Enthusiastic

Love You

I miss you more always then I can say
I have so much more to say and always so little time to say how + What I feel. I would Make you so happy + I would Never Cheat on you. I wish you felt the way I do about you but I Know you don't.

P.S.   Sorry so sloppy
Love ya always

"Why the hell would he give this to you?" I asked. "Why would he think… what did he say? *You might need it?* Why would you need it? Just to destroy me? As if I haven't been destroyed enough already? And you! Why did you even show this to me?!!"

"I'm sorry. I didn't know what to do. I thought you'd want to know."

"You know what, Mom, I am boiling mad right now, and I have no idea how to deal with this. I've got to leave. I can't believe this is happening."

"Steve, please stay. You're too upset to drive."

I hesitated for a minute. She was right. I shouldn't be driving in a state of mind like this.

"Okay, you're right." I asked if she'd make some coffee.

While she made a pot of coffee and set out a plate of cookies, Macadamia nut, my favorite, I went down into the basement.

It stank of urine, mold and cigarettes. The furniture was worn out, and there was filth and dust everywhere. There were empty rum bottles strewn about, piles of trash and fast food wrappers everywhere. In the bathroom, the vanity was rusted, rotted and in pieces on the floor. Everything was covered with mold and mildew. The smell forced me back up the stairs.

Halfway up, I caught sight of a prescription bottle. I went back down, picked it up, thinking, "Let's see how sick, my evil brother really is." As I read the label, I didn't know whether to laugh or cry.

It was a prescription for Viagra! In some way, this made me feel better. After all, he was only 39 years old, and I was glad to see that his toxic lifestyle had taken its toll. I shook the bottle and found nothing in it. But wait, there *was* something. I opened the bottle to find a piece of paper with Angie's name and cell phone number on it.

CHAPTER 19
A STRANGE INTERLUDE

THAT AUGUST, after Angie left for Baltimore, grieving my lost son continued to consume nearly all my energy. Angie and Jodi being gone took something out of me as well. In addition, the cold response I received from everyone at work sucked the life out of me. It felt as if I was getting hit from every angle.

I also now felt the hatred of the guys who worked for the Mason Baking Company, a rival to the company I worked for. Any time I encountered one of them, they'd stare me down as though they were ready for a fight. But they never approached me. I eventually learned that Jim Watkins worked for Mason part-time.

Several months after Angie's departure, I saw Jim Watkins at one of the K-Stores on my route. He was dressed in the exact same outfit that Angie had once bought for me. After a brief look at me, he turned sideways, and slipped away.

Of course I didn't think he'd have anything to say to me—I would've been an idiot to expect an apology; I certainly wasn't going to confront him—no good would have come of it. I considered him a stupid, lowlife punk, but it was foolish of me to blame him for the affair. It was Angie's fault, too, probably more so, because honoring our marriage had been *her* responsibility, not his.

Seeing him made me angry again at Angie, not just for cheating on me, but for using my money—our children's money—to buy clothes and who knows what else for that goofy-looking bastard.

Mom reminded me again to keep my temper under control, "Please tell me you won't hurt him."

"I give you my word, Mom. I just have to avoid him."

The next day, while chatting at K-Stores with my friend Lydia who managed the store's deliveries, I mentioned I had seen my wife's former boyfriend, delivering for the Mason Baking Company. I told Lydia that I'd been trying my best to avoid the mess my wife had created, but now here was one of her former lovers, right in my face, in my workplace. It seemed cruel and spiteful that Watkins had begun to service a store that he knew was part of my business. Lydia agreed, and advised me to talk with the store manager, Velma Rollins. So that's exactly what I did.

I explained that I was having a hard enough time dealing with what had happened without having to see someone partially responsible for the disaster during my workday. Velma said she'd take care of it.

I thanked her, finished work, and went to the cemetery. When I got home I received a call from one of my bosses who asked me to meet her the next day at a restaurant in Concord. I had never met with her off site before, and I had a bad feeling.

My boss, accompanied by her boss, met with me the next day. They'd received another report from the K-Store that Velma Rollins managed. This report accused me of sexually harassing my friend Lydia.

In exchange for not pressing charges, K-Stores had banned me from ever stepping foot in their stores again, even as a customer. K-Stores was one of my company's biggest customers; losing that store meant that I was out of business.

My bosses stressed that no one would be pressing charges, as long as I did not try to pursue any legal action.

"I can't fight," I said. "I've been beaten enough. But thank you, because everything, including this job, is just too much, and I'm glad to be free of it."

After all of the papers were signed, all I could think was: *There has to be more to this. Why would K-Stores set me up like this? Did Jim Watkins have something to do with it?*

Mom was upset to hear that I'd lost my business and that I was banned from K-Stores. She knew, of course, that I had never sexually harassed anyone, especially Lydia. Together we tried to understand why K-Stores would go to such lengths to get rid of me.

While we were talking, Angie called. This was the first time I'd talked to her since she'd left four months ago. It seemed odd that she'd call today of all days, and even odder that she asked specifically how work was going. When I told her I'd lost my job that very day, she said, "You lost your job because of your big mouth."

"What the hell is that supposed to mean, Angie?"

"Forget it...just forget it," she said in her usual way.

"You can't just throw something like that at me and then not explain it. What the hell do you mean I lost my job because of my big mouth?"

"Forget it, Steve. And don't tell me what I can or can't say."

"Why the hell are you calling me today, Angie? You must know something about this, and about your boyfriend being there, so how about you just tell me what it is so I can be prepared for the next disaster that's going to happen."

"Stop being so damned suspicious. I'm just calling because I care."

As if I'd ever believe that. "Goodbye, Angie," I said and hung up.

—·—

With no job, no family and few friends, I developed the habit of walking around town, recalling happier times when Angie and the kids and I would walk around and drop into a restaurant. Those seemed like good memories, but I knew now that the happiness I had experienced then had been an illusion; I'd been living in a world of lies from the day I met her.

During one of my walks I stopped at a little tavern and ordered a beer. I felt guilty for treating myself to anything when my son could not sit beside me, and I tried not to cry with every sip. I felt alone, scared, and confused about where life had taken me. After about 30 minutes the bartender asked if I wanted another beer.

"No thanks, one is my limit."

"Don't look so sad." A very pretty woman with jet black hair smiled at me. "You're too good-looking to be that sad."

"Sorry if I disturbed you," I said. "I'm getting ready to leave anyway."

"You can't leave without at least telling me your name."

I thought it was strange that she didn't know who I was. Surely everyone in town knew who I was by then. "My name is Steve, but I have to go."

She moved closer. "You seem like a nice guy, but you're not much of a gentleman."

I just looked at her.

"My name is Maryanne," she said. "You could have at least asked me my name."

"I'm sorry. I didn't mean to be rude. I have a lot on my mind."

"Well maybe we can sort it out together," she said.

It had been years since a woman had approached me like this. Not since Angie. But for some reason, I found myself opening up a little. "Something very bad has happened to me, and I'm lost. I don't know where I am in life, I don't know where I'm going, and I don't even know who I am anymore."

"It sounds to me like you need a friend. I'll be your friend. Would you like to come to my house and talk?"

It was quite the come-on, and of course I was flattered. But I was also suspicious. "Please forgive me, but I don't even know you," I said. "You seem like a very nice lady, but then again so did my wife. And I'm not interested in any new friendships with women right now."

"I *am* a very nice lady, I don't know what your wife did to you, but maybe I can help."

"Maryanne, I don't think you have the help I need. Thank you very much, but I can't talk anymore. It's time for me to go."

I got up to leave, and she got up, too.

"We don't have to talk. I'll just walk with you."

"Maryanne, believe me, you don't want to go where I'm going."

I left the tavern and drove to the cemetery, where I got down on my hands and knees and cried uncontrollably. I found comfort crying like that because it felt as though I was destroying myself when I did. Some part of me just disappeared, and it was the part that was battered and wounded and broken. The crying and the pain felt as if that the most real part of me; the part I could give most deeply to Chub, short of taking my own life.

I struggled to my feet and dragged myself to the parking lot where a black Mercedes was now parked behind my truck. As I got closer, the Mercedes door opened and out stepped Maryanne.

"I'm sorry for intruding. I just wanted to talk to you."

She'd followed me. I wondered how long had she been there. I didn't know whether to get upset because someone had violated what I considered my sacred place, or to welcome her as a friend. "What can I do for you, Maryanne?"

"Can I say a prayer?"

I was not expecting this, and it was such a kind gesture that I said, "Of course."

She walked over to the grave, made the sign of the cross, bowed her head, and said, "Your last name is Tenaglia?"

"Yes, but that's my father's grave. If you want to say another prayer, do it over the next grave, two steps over."

She moved to Chub's grave, and froze. She made the sign of the cross again, looked into my eyes, and said, "I am so sorry."

"Thank you for your prayers Maryanne, but I have to go home now."

She asked, "Where do you live? Let me spend some time with you."

She seemed sincere and caring. "I live about two miles up the road. If you like, you can follow me."

She told me how nice my house was. I said it was a nice enough house, but not much of a home. Explaining that my wife had not put any love into it began a conversation that lasted for hours. Maryanne and her husband had both taught at the same school, but he'd left her for one another teacher. Though I was sorry to hear her story, it also comforted me. Here was someone who knew the pain I'd experienced with Angie.

We became friends, but I absolutely did not want a relationship. This put some stress on our friendship because she clearly wanted more. We joined each other almost every day for coffee and conversation. Mostly we talked about how badly our spouses had hurt us. She told me about ways she was trying to get back at her husband. At the same time she told me how good-looking I was and how much she liked me. Her intensity scared me. She was on some type of disability and wasn't working, and I worried that she might want to take advantage of me financially.

Then early one morning, while I was still in bed, she called to let me know she was on her way with breakfast. She'd already arrived by the time I got up. As I walked down the hall to the kitchen, I noticed that she had placed dozens of sticky notes on every wall in my house. They said things like, "I'm so lucky that I met you," and "My life is so wonderful now that you're part of it," and, "Do you have any idea how good-looking you are?" She'd even written a letter to me *from my son*.

Now I was really frightened.

There she was, all bubbly and full of energy, with breakfast laid out on the table. She asked if I would go with her to the Beerings' party the following weekend.

"Maryanne, I'm not ready to socialize. I really don't want to be around people. I'm in a lot of emotional pain, and I would feel guilty having a good time when I know that my son cannot."

But she wasn't going to take no for an answer.

"You need to get out of the house and have some fun, Steve. It's okay for you to start living again. Do you think little Steve would want you to be so isolated and alone? And besides, the Beerings are very nice people. Sean Harrison, who also will be there, is the mayor of Mount Pleasant. He owns practically everything in town. It would be good to mingle with these folks. Please come with me."

Again I declined. I was not the least bit interested in meeting anyone.

The next day Maryanne came over again, and all she talked about was the Beerings and their big party. She carried on and on and on, while I pleaded for her to stop and respect my decision to stay home and go to the cemetery, which were the only two things that interested me. I said that I didn't want to ruin the party with my sadness and tears.

But she wouldn't give up. "It's okay, Steve. They would understand. Many of them are professionals in the medical field. If anything they could help you." She paused for a second. "Besides, I've already told them all about you, and they want to meet you."

I told her I'd think about it, and for the next two days that was all she talked about. I heard about the food, music, entertainment, the doctors and lawyers that would be there and how spectacular this shindig was going to be. Nothing could have been less interesting to me.

Persistence and dedication are the tools for success. Being a woman is also helpful when trying to convince a man to do something. Long story short, I ended up going to the party.

There was nothing fun about that party. I was stuck in my own little world thinking about nothing but the death of my son, invisible to all the people around me. Occasionally I'd peek out and see Maryanne fluttering around talking and laughing, obviously having a very good time. And then I'd retreat into my own world again. Eventually she asked if I wanted something to eat, and led me over to the grill where Mayor Harrison was cooking.

Maryanne introduced us. He glared at me, tossed a burger and a hotdog on my plate, and then looked away without saying a word. As Maryanne and I walked to a table with our plates, I asked, "What was his problem? He seemed really rude."

"Oh, you've got to get to know Sean," she said. "That's just his personality."

I'd had enough of this party and wanted to leave, and she agreed it was time to go. We drove back to my house and she apologized. We agreed to talk the next day.

The next day I called Maryanne and there was no answer. After about an hour I dropped by her place. Her car was in the driveway so I knew she was home, but after ringing the doorbell a few times, there was no answer. I thought she might be in the shower or something, so I went to the store to get a cup of coffee and then went back to her house. This time while ringing the doorbell, a police car pulled into the driveway and an officer got out. He asked me for my identification and asked what I was doing there. I told him Maryanne was my friend and we'd agreed to get together that morning. Since she hadn't answered her phone I came by because I was concerned about her.

The officer knocked on the door and Maryanne appeared. She did not look at me, but let the officer in while I waited on the porch. After about five minutes the officer came out and said "Maryanne doesn't want to see you."

It was a strange thing to happen, but honestly I was relieved. I'd had my fill of Maryanne by this point.

"Thank you," I said to the officer.

As he handed me my license back he said, "I told her that you were concerned about her, and she said that you were too controlling."

I said, "Does that mean she isn't going to bother *me* anymore?"

I was never so happy to have a woman break up with me. But ... she accused me of being *controlling*. That's the same thing Angie had always said. Why would Maryanne say that, too? I'd never done anything to encourage her to think of herself as my girlfriend, and we'd never had an argument, other than her pressuring me to go to that awful party.

Why would a woman who blatantly came on to me, who followed me to the cemetery, papered my house with post-it notes and begged me for three days to go to a party with her, suddenly refuse to see me, saying that *I'm* controlling? What had happened between yesterday and today?

Nothing other than the party.

It occurred to me that Jim Watkins and the Beerings might be somehow linked. It was a small town, and a lot of people were related in one way or another. If Harrison connected who I was at the party, he must have then told Maryanne the stories that were going around, and that was the end of that. The rumors had now reached even into the upper crust of Concord/Mt. Pleasant society.

Another possibility might be that my grief and isolation were causing me to become paranoid and more than a little psychotic. I am still not sure.

CHAPTER 20
NOT DEAD, BUT NOT ALIVE

AROUND THIS TIME I learned that Angie had also had a long-term affair with a state trooper, the same guy who I'd seen at the McDonald's playground at Myrtle Beach—the same man she was with in a motel room while leaving our kids unsupervised at the pool.

I reported this to the police.

Naturally there was nothing they could do. No laws had been broken. But while I talked to the deputy, he let it slip that Angie had called the police numerous times over the last couple of years with complaints about me.

I had no knowledge of this; I'd never been questioned or arrested. I was curious what those complaints said and went to the Police Department to ask. The sergeant on duty claimed there were no records there. When I pushed the matter, he finally conceded that Angie had filed many complaints against me. It appeared that she had been creating a paper trail that would substantiate her later claims that I had been beating her and abusing the kids.

It was a brilliant strategy on her part, and of course I didn't want it on my record. A friend told me that I had a right to see my public records, which would include all 911 calls about me, so, with nothing but time on my hands, I set about to get those records. I went to three different police departments and the District Attorney. Each one promised to give me the records, but none ever materialized. I finally called the State's Attorney and the F.B.I., but got no response. I came to believe that Angie had something to do with those records being hidden, and also with the police refusing to respond to the five reports I filed about my vending machines being vandalized and stolen.

At the end of August, I had to go to court to enforce what I will refer to as the *Decorum extortion promissory contract*. After two years of waiting for my original down payment to be returned, I learned that Darren Long, the man who had bought my Decorum franchise, was now suing me for an additional $110,000. This was after he had put me out of business, costing me around a half a million dollars.

Knowing that I was still an emotional wreck, my lawyer placed me in a separate room while he faced Long and his lawyer.

My lawyer came into the room where I waited serveral times with questions. One question quickly brought me out of my stupor.

"Long says he called you asking for help, but you didn't help him," my attorney said. "Why not?"

"He's lying. He never called me. Subpoena his phone records and you'll see that he has never dialed my number."

Shortly after that my attorney returned and said that Long had agreed to pay me a settlement. After spending five years building a successful business that was virtually stolen from me, I was now going to receive a pittance.

Now my anger matched my grief in its intensity, and it did not let up. In fact, it continued to worsen.

I could not retaliate against Angie and Jim Watkins, or Long, or the people at K-Stores, or anybody.

Instead, I started screaming at the devil himself. Screaming, crying, driving, every day, for hours, I continued this angry rampage for forty days.

During this phase, I stopped at a convenience store in my neighborhood. A woman took one look at me and said, "You've got to go to the doctor, right away."

I ignored her and she said again, "You need to get to the doctor," pointing to my leg. It was a hot day and I was wearing shorts, but I had not noticed the big black blister on my leg. It was the size of a goose egg.

"You've been bitten by a brown recluse spider and if you don't go the hospital, you could lose that leg."

My doctor saw me immediately and made arrangements for me to be admitted to the hospital, where several doctors took a look at my leg. I was told that I needed immediate surgery, but I didn't think it was a big deal.

I was oblivious to everything—the world around me, the people I'd worked with and even my own body. Nothing made an impression on me.

I woke up from surgery with a bandage wrapped around my calf. Beneath the bandage was an egg-sized hole that reached all the way down to the bone.

Staff agreed with the woman in the convenience store. If I had have waited another day there was a good chance my leg would have been amputated.

I stayed in the hospital for about five days, angrier than ever.

After I was released, I drove my car around town screaming out loud at the spider, at Satan, at Angie, at Long, at Jim Watkins, at everybody, and at nobody in particular... at God.

Haven't you done enough to me? Come on and stand in front of me, you punk. You even attacked me with a spider! Why? Why? Why? If you're supposed to be so tough and have so much power, then why are you afraid to stand in front of me? Or talk to me? Or explain this to me? What else have you got? What are you going to do to me next?

It was coming up on a year since Chub's death and I felt guilty that my grief wasn't as intense as it had been originally. Mom said this was a natural part of the healing process. She told me not to feel guilty for feeling less pain, because that's not what my little boy would want. She'd been through the same thing after my father's death, and she urged me to find some grief counseling.

I didn't want to bring a stranger into my private world of pain. All I wanted to do was go to the cemetery and cry for my boy.

In addition to spending hours at the cemetery, I also spent time just driving around, trying to figure out what happened to my life.

I had made it easy for my wife to walk away from the aftermath of the accident, basically unscathed. Why had I pleaded for her to be released from jail and given community service rather than a prison sentence?

It made me an accomplice, defending her and protecting her even though I knew how awful she was.

Instead of blaming her for the affair with my brother, I had blamed *him,* which was ridiculous, because he was just as vulnerable to her manipulations as every other man who crossed her path.

But why had I lost my business, not once, but twice? Why did people in town stare at me? Why had Maryanne called the police on me?

I was convinced Angie was a witch with evil powers, and had cursed my entire life.

I have no idea how long this insane behavior continued. A few weeks maybe? A few months? I had no sense of time. I vaguely recall my mom trying to help me, talking to me, trying to comfort me, and pleading with me to see a counselor, to get some help.

But I ignored her advice. All I did every day was drive to the cemetery and workout.

In December, during one of my angry driving trips, on a straight stretch of road doing 55 MPH, I cried so intensely that I had to wipe the tears from my eyes. I felt my body shake as I leaned to the right, and I heard what sounded like a spraying of heavy rain on the outside of my SUV. I felt a thud in my stomach and a crunching in my chest, and at the same time there was a quick, cracking sound and a gush in my head. As I moved my hands away from my face, I realized that the seat and I were pressed up against the dashboard and my head was where the mirror used to be, up against the windshield. It took what seemed like several minutes before I realized what had happened.

I unbuckled my seatbelt and tried to pull myself away from the dashboard, but it felt as though the right side of my head was glued to the windshield. So again I tried to move away from the windshield, and I lifted myself up a bit, but this time, while pulling my head to the left, I felt a shock of pain, and I heard and felt something like a "slurp." So I turned my head to the right to see where the weird slurping sound came from, and saw it was the two-inch piece of metal that held the mirror to the windshield. I had just pulled it out of my head!

I felt something dripping down the side of my face, which I assumed was blood, but when I reached my hand up to wipe it off, it wasn't blood at all. It was a warm, clear liquid. Rather than sitting there trying to figure out what this stuff was, I decided it was more important to get out of my truck, so I wiped my hand on my pants and tried to open the door, but it would only open about eight inches. I had to kick it several times, and finally it opened enough for me crawl out. I climbed up an embankment and there was a police officer.

All I remember after that was the ground coming up and slamming me in the face.

I was taken by helicopter from Rowan Regional Hospital to North Carolina Baptist Hospital, a level one trauma center. The diagnoses included severe closed head injury, bruising to both lungs with deflation, and multiple rib fractures. Tubes were placed in my chest to re-expand my lungs. CT exams revealed blood in the space around both lungs, and I was in acute respiratory failure with oxygen levels dropping into the 80s and a drastic drop in blood pressure to 60/40.

I am now walking effortlessly through a dark tunnel. I am lost, with no fear as to where I am going, I continue walking. Although it is very dark, I can see there is an end to this tunnel.

I remained unconscious for five weeks. A blood clot formed in my right lung and I was diagnosed with Adult Respiratory Distress Syndrome. They plugged me full of tubes, pumped me full of drugs, and repeatedly sent me back to the operating room to patch things up as each organ fell apart, beginning with the lungs, then the bowels, and an eventual diagnosis of sepsis — an infection in my blood – and pneumonia. I hovered somewhere between this world and the next, kept alive by technology, facing one complication after another.

I get through the tunnel, and am now standing in a huge, very dark field, and way off in the distance are these tiny, very bright lights, almost like an airfield at night. I walk toward these little lights and notice that they are getting bigger and brighter.

I finally reach these lights. They are about three and a half feet tall and facing me. They go as far as I can see to my left and as far as I can see to my right. There is nothing but silence, but there is a movement behind these lights.

I made several more trips to the operating room; surgeons repaired my lacerated liver, inserted a feeding tube, put me on a ventilator, and operated on my obstructed bowel. I had a fractured cheekbone, and both shoulder blades were fractured, but my brain appeared to be intact.

I am about 15 feet away from these lights, and take a few more steps to see what is behind this wall of lights. I am now about arm's length away, and am able to see rows and rows of people standing in lines, which seems like miles long, as far as I can see. No one spoke. Everyone had on gray robes with hoods over their heads. All I can see are their profiles. I can't tell if they are men or women. There is no sound, so I just stand there and watch.

After some time the lines move. Everyone takes a step forward and continues to wait in silence. All of a sudden off to my right, about the length of a football field away, I hear a terribly frightening scream...a scream of horror. Something has happened! As I look over this sea of people, the lines move again, just one step, in silence.

I stay outside this wall of lights for a long time. It's impossible to say how long, because time feels different here. There is no daylight, there is no night, and there is no time, just a silent waiting with an occasional dreadful, horrifying scream.

By New Year's Day, 2004, my heart and lungs had stabilized and I was removed from life support.

Suddenly I was awake, immediately aware that I was in a hospital. I tried to ask, "Where am I?" but I couldn't talk. I couldn't move my head, my arms or my legs. I couldn't move at all. I was strapped to the bed, sitting in an upright position. I heard the doctors and nurses tell me that I was very lucky. I did not feel lucky.

I had no recollection of what happened.

After two days I was able to speak. I told a nurse that all I could remember was driving to the cemetery and wiping my eyes while I was crying.

When doctors came to see me I would ask, "Why didn't you let me go? Why did you have to save me?" I'd cry over missing my chance to be with little Steve and they'd tell me that I should be thankful to be alive, that not many people could have survived my injuries. They told me that my strong, muscular body helped to save me. And they told me again how lucky I was.

I didn't feel lucky. I had tubes coming out of every orifice in my body. All I could think was that I had to get back to the cemetery.

My mom and sister came to visit and I asked, "How bad am I?"

"The doctors did not expect you to make it," my mom said. "We came to see you every day while you were in your coma, and we prayed for you."

I asked again, "Tell me the truth. How badly was I hurt?"

"You broke your skull and punctured your brain. You broke your temple, your cheek, both shoulders, your clavicle, and I don't know how many ribs, though I think I heard a doctor say it was eleven. Both your lungs were punctured, and many of your organs were damaged. One doctor told me that there was no way you could live through this, and I told him that I *knew* you would make it, because after everything you'd been through, this could not be the way your life ends."

I continued to improve, and over the next couple of weeks my body began to start healing on its own. The liver laceration was no longer visible on x-rays. My rib and facial fractures, along with the major head trauma, slowly mended. My lungs were beginning to heal, even though I still had pneumonia.

Near the end of February, 2004, with the help of the doctors and nurses, physical therapy and the good grace of God, I was discharged. I stayed in bed at Mom's house for the next five months. At first I was only able to get up out of bed for one minute at a time.

My primary care physician gave me a morphine patch and oxycodone for the pain, and a drug called Mobic that he said would help with my healing. Then he prescribed Klonapin to stop my shaking because of the nerve damage, and Zoloft to help with my depression. As he prescribed each drug, he explained in explicit detail how it would help me.

On my second doctor's appointment, I was still in terrible pain, but it was more tolerable. While I waited in the exam room, I peeked into my medical chart, and to my surprise there was a sticky note on top of my chart which read, "This patient yells and screams and uses profanity, and also uses threatening language on the phone when calling the office. The staff is afraid of him."

I showed this to the doctor when he came in, and he just shrugged and threw it into the garbage. I told him in a whisper, "I am recuperating from two collapsed lungs, and I could not yell and scream if I tried. I can barely walk, and barely move. I'm not in any physical condition to threaten anyone. What is this about?"

"It's nothing. Don't worry about it."

I didn't have the strength to question this. I trusted him. I just left it alone.

The third time I went to see the doctor I was sitting in a wheelchair near the open door of the exam room when a redheaded nurse passed by. She stopped and looked at me with such hatred that it scared me. It seemed that I'd seen her somewhere before.

When the doctor came into the room, he acted cold and distant. I asked if he would prescribe some topical Silvadene for the fourteen-inch long wound on my stomach, and he said "No more drugs."

"Doctor," I said, "I think I can make it without the pain medicine, but I still need to heal, and I still have the shakes. Can you…"

"No more drugs. I'll give you Ultracet and send you to the pain clinic." And he left.

His rudeness left me confused and I did not know what to do, so I decided to get out of there as fast as I could.

With only about five percent mobility in my left arm, I wheeled my chair directly into the left side of the doorway. I pulled back on the right wheel to straighten myself out, and pushed as fast and hard as I could with my left hand and made it into the hallway. I tried to maneuver the chair so that I could progress down the hall, but I smacked into the wall. Nobody was around to help me and I begin to panic. I pushed and pushed trying to move the chair, but the more I pushed, the more unbearable the pain became, and soon I was screaming in anguish.

Eventually I made it back to the waiting room where my mom and sister wheeled me out and helped me into the car. And while I calmed down with their help, the pain raged, and I begged God to let me die. But he didn't let me die, so I just sat in the back seat moaning and crying.

A few days later, after further aggravating my injuries, I called the doctor's office. The receptionist told me that their office would no longer see me.

"Why?" I asked.

"You asked for prescription drugs on your last visit."

"May I please speak to my doctor?"

"No. We will no longer be treating you."

"Well that's fine, but can I please be referred to the pain clinic?"

"No," she said and hung up.

I took the Ultracet as the doctor had prescribed, but soon felt terribly sick. About six hours I asked my sister to drive me to the store so I could buy *The Pill Book*. I looked up Ultracet. The book said Ultracet should not be prescribed to patients with head injuries or head trauma.

I stayed in bed for the next four days in pain and wondering again what the hell went wrong. Mom advised me to try to get by without medication because I would heal faster without it, and that whenever the pain got to be unbearable, just think about my son.

I had nothing to do but stay in bed, endure the pain, and think about my life. Surely there was some sort of evil force working against me.

I began to put some of the pieces together. I remembered where I had seen the redheaded nurse. She was a Harrison; I'd seen her at the party. I figured she was the one who had turned Maryanne against me, and now she had convinced my doctor to turn me away as well.

Laying in bed, I began to recall things I'd heard about Angie, things I'd blocked from my memory, such as the story about a K-Stores assistant manager named Bill Smith who had sex with her in his office. As many stories as I heard about her, I suspect she spread just as many about me. There were so many stories, so many possible truths and lies, that I couldn't figure it out in ten lifetimes.

It had been two years since my son's death. I was still partially crippled from my accident and the pain was still indescribable, but it was nothing compared to the loss of my son.

The extent of my injuries meant that I was not physically able to run another business. One doctor estimated that I had sustained 25% brain damage. I was clearly having trouble with my memory.

Still, I wanted to work so I enrolled in an eight-week college course in Florida to learn how to become a train conductor. A passing grade for the class was 85%, and although I got 92.3 (the lowest in the class), it just about killed me. I had to read things six and seven times to retain the information.

I returned from Florida, and my mother and sister were proud that I passed and that I could now find a job. They both kept encouraging me, telling me what a huge success I was for accomplishing this, despite my disabilities.

I didn't feel like a success.

— · —

In January, 2005, Angie called to ask how I was doing. I told her that I was doing as well as could be expected, considering all that had happened.

Though I still felt like yelling at her for killing our son, and for ruining my life, I knew it would be pointless. Instead, I barely said a word, acting as cold and neutral as I possibly could. I was interested to hear news about Jodi. She told me that Jodi was giving her a hard time because she wanted to have a boyfriend. The thought of that sweet girl following in her mother's footsteps made me feel ill. I asked if I could talk to her, but Angie said she would have Jodi call me later.

Jodi never called, but a few weeks later Angie called again. This time it was to tell me that she was probably going to go to jail. I asked why, and she replied with her usual, "Never mind, just forget it."

I asked again, "What did you do now?"

"I've ruined my life. I'm just a fuck-up."

"Yes you are a fuck-up, but you ruined your life a long time ago, and a lot of other people's lives along the way. So what evil, sick thing did you do this time? Is Jodi okay?"

Then she said, "I have to go," and hung up.

I started to worry about Jodi. I was so worried for her safety that the next morning I went to Baltimore to find out what had happened. I drove for six hours, straight to the Howard County Courthouse. There I asked the district attorney if Jodi was alright. The DA asked me for some identification, so I showed her my license and a newspaper clipping about how Angie had killed our son. I told her that I was worried about Jodi's safety.

After checking their records, the DA informed me that Angie and Jodi did not live in Howard County.

Angie had lied to me again. I asked the DA to please run a statewide search for both Angie and Jodi. I gave her my cell phone number and drove into the city of Baltimore.

Within the hour, I received a call from the DA's office. Jodi had been severely beaten by her mother. They wanted to know how I knew about this before the paperwork was even done, and I told them that I'd received a call from Angie saying that she might go to jail, but she wouldn't tell me why. I just had an eerie feeling that Jodi was in danger. They told me that Angie and Jodi lived about sixty miles away in Harford County, and asked if I would drive up to Harford County Courthouse.

There I met with someone from the District Attorney's Office. He told me that Jodi's teachers at school had noticed bruises and had contacted the local police. I gave him a copy of the newspaper story about the accident. I also told him about Angie's affairs, her lies, and all the other things she'd done. He was attentive and understanding. He had two children of his own, and assured me he would do everything he could to see that Jodi was safe.

I drove back home to North Carolina and later heard from the DA's office that the felony charges had been dropped against Angie. Jodi's injuries were not life-threatening and she had been placed in a foster home. I couldn't believe that Angie got away with another crime, especially since she was on probation. The DA's office told me that the law could only do so much because the injuries that Jodi sustained would cause no permanent damage.

"*No permanent damage?* You mean to tell me a little girl who lost her baby brother and then her dad within a few months, and gets beat up with bruises so bad that her teachers reported it to the police, then gets put into foster care, has no permanent damage? I'm a grown man, and *I'm* permanently damaged from the things that woman did to me. Jodi's just a kid. How will she ever recover from this?"

"As long as there's no permanent damage to her body, they have to reduce the charges. It's the law. But a misdemeanor charge still violates Angie's probation, and I assure you, we take assault on a child very seriously."

What happened over the next several months was typical of everything Angie had ever been involved in.

She went to court in May and asked for a jury trial. At the pre-trial, in June, Jodi changed her story, saying that the bruises were caused by a bunch of kids at school who beat her with a baseball bat. The DA knew this was a lie, but dropped the case because Jodi needed a home and a mother. Once again, Angie, a woman who had left one of her children on a doorstep, killed another one, and beat up a third, was off the hook. This time she'd worked her magic by getting Jodi to change her story. Not only had Jodi lost any sense of safety and security, she had also lost her dignity and self-esteem.

In our divorce agreement, Angie was required to relinquish my last name, because I did not want any further association with her, even if it was in name only. She agreed to not use my last name again, but as usual, she lied. Because when she beat up Jodi, she was arrested as Angie Tenaglia.

CHAPTER 21
DEALING WITH PAIN

FALL OF 2005, nearly three years after the death of my son, an old friend, David, whom I hadn't seen since my son's funeral, stopped by to visit. We had known each other through work, but since he had been single and I had been married during most of the time we knew each other, we hadn't spent much time together. He first apologized for not coming to see me sooner. "I figured you needed more time."

I thanked him, and while I explained to him about the unbelievably absurd catastrophes that had occurred, I broke down.

With genuine concern he said, "You have to calm down, Steve. Are you on some sort of medication? Is there something you can take to help you calm down?"

I said my doctor had refused to continue treating me and confessed that I just wanted to die.

"There are good doctors out there, and you need to find one. You need help."

I lost my temper. "I don't need help!" I shouted. "I don't trust anyone. I can deal with the pain just fine. I like my pain. It keeps me in touch with reality."

"What do you mean?"

"It's this pain that torments me into knowing I'm alive."

"Hey, Steve, you really need some help. No doctor should turn you away. If your doctor really did that, then you need to find another one. Maybe even report this guy for malpractice. But right now, you need some help."

Again I yelled at him, "I don't know where to go, and I can't take anymore let downs, so I'm just going to stay in bed and try to heal."

"You won't heal that way. You can't just lie in bed being angry at the world. If there's anything I can do for you, even just to talk, call me. I'm not a doctor, but you need to calm down."

He reached into his pocket and pulled out something that looked like a cigarette case. "Take a hit of this joint later, and maybe it will help."

The gift my friend gave me that day kept me calm enough so that I could function more or less normally instead of constantly dwelling on my rage and grief.

After a few calmer days I made an appointment with the pain clinic. I filled out all the necessary paperwork. From my neck to my waist, from shoulder to shoulder, all the way to my spine, was one big bruise. Every breath I took was painful. Every step I took was excruciating and irritated the 14-inch, raw-looking wound that went from my chest to two inches below where my navel used to be.

My first visit to the pain clinic was a nightmare. A doctor came into the room with the same look on her face that I received from everybody else in town. She had heard the rumors, had read my medical records, and was biased against me. She asked about my pain and I told her, "I had a bad car accident about two years ago and I feel like one big bruise."

She asked me, "Where do you feel like this big bruise?"

Because of my injuries, I couldn't reach up to point to my shoulders, so I pointed toward *her* shoulders to show her where it hurt.

She jumped back and snapped, "Don't touch me!" She told me to take Tylenol or Motrin for the pain and to make another appointment, and then had a nurse come in to draw my blood.

On my next visit, the doctor exhibited a different attitude. She smiled, but her smile was more like a smirk, and I felt uneasy about her now-exaggerated niceness. My visit was short and a lot more professional, but in the end she didn't give me any medication for pain, and she put a red flag on my medical record for marijuana use, which I assume had showed up on my blood test.

One day I was walking down Union Street when I noticed a black woman staring at me. She was staring at me like she knew me, but she did not look familiar.

"Excuse me," I said. "Do I know you?"

"I was in jail with your wife."

I asked how her life was going now that she was out of jail.

She said, "I'm all right; I'm trying to get a job. Where is Angie now? Have you heard from her?"

I told her Angie had moved to Baltimore and was on probation.

"Your wife seemed like a nice lady, but she said something that I just didn't understand. When I asked what she was in for, she said, 'I killed my husband's son.'"

Angie hadn't even claimed Steve as her own child?

She continued, "I stayed away from her because she just didn't seem right in the head." I asked her if Angie ever cried in jail, and she said, "Oh no, she was always very calm and cool. She never seemed to have any feelings at all."

CHAPTER 22
LOST IN THE FOG OF ANGER

EVERY DAY, both physically and mentally, I felt worse. I was wide awake, but at the same time, immersed in a dark, slimy fog. I couldn't remember little things like people's names, names of streets, or why I had gone to the store.

All I could think about, all day long, was how Angie and her boyfriends had destroyed my life. Anger had become part of my body, constantly present, in every breath, in every waking moment.

One day a letter arrived from the plastic surgery center that had done Angie's breast implants. They were letting patients know that the doctor had been accused of taking "immoral liberties" with his patients. For a moment I wondered if he was the one who had started Angie on her twisted path, or whether Angie had corrupted *him*?

I had lost faith in mankind and had become completely paranoid. When I went out in public I looked over my shoulder to see who might be watching me so I could be aware enough to meet evil head-on the next time it found me. I questioned everyone who spoke to me. They all seemed evil, and I didn't trust any of them, because there was no way for me to know if this person or that person had been involved in Angie's lies. Every man I saw was a suspect… had he slept with my wife? Every woman was a potential gossip monger. I wasn't safe anywhere. I felt as if I was being watched all the time, and was just waiting for something else to happen.

I was more like a wounded animal than a living human being. I had reached the point that I could not bear to hear any more bad news or stories of the evil around me. I stayed home and didn't want to leave. I was safe in my home, and I got to the point where my only contact with the world was by mail and telephone, but I didn't use my phone much, and I didn't open my mail.

I had couple of friends, Eric and Derrick, who didn't mind me crying without reservation and expressing my true feelings about the loss of my boy. I also confided in my mom and my sister, who would listen with open minds, but were horrified to hear about my feelings and my lost sense of reality.

To be honest, it had to be difficult for anyone to talk to me. I no longer talked to people in a normal voice. Instead, I screamed.

I remember Mom telling me to stop yelling, and I screamed at her, trying to convince her that I wasn't yelling. I tried to explain to her that I was too exhausted to yell, but she told me again and again that I was yelling. When I realized that I could not even communicate with my own mother, I descended further inside myself, because now even my mother seemed afraid of me.

Then one evening I met a woman just walking the street, and she seemed as dazed, dysfunctional and lost as I was. Her name was Valerie, and I could feel her sorrow. She told me she'd recently lost her husband to cancer and she was devastated.

We began confiding in each other, sharing our war stories and our feelings of loss and anguish. We analyzed the reasons why we felt so crippled by sorrow, and she seemed to understand me. She heard the questions that haunted me.

Unlike others, Valerie was not afraid of me. There was no wall between us, and although she was a very attractive female, she was more like a fellow human stuck in the foxhole of grief and loss. It seemed as though she as reaching in to help pull me out of my darkness, but I was too far gone, and

I knew she couldn't really help. But it was good to talk to her.

One day, I said (screamed), "Valerie, I can't handle this anymore! Even my mother is frightened of me."

"First of all," Valerie said, "stop yelling at everyone. Your mom is going through the same thing you are. She lost her only grandchild and almost lost you. Don't you think that she's hurting too? She's a strong lady, but she is fighting with this also. She doesn't have to be strong just for you; she has to be strong for herself, too. Yelling at your mom is wrong, Steve."

"Valerie, I was not yelling. I would never yell at my mom. That's just the way I talk now. My anger makes my words come out as screams, because that's how I feel inside."

"Then you need to change. You cannot continue to live like this. Start by calling your mom and apologizing to her right now. "

She was right, of course, so I called Mom and apologized.

A few days later I woke up in a panic to get to the cemetery. I rushed out of the house and on my way there got pulled over by the police. They cited me for crossing the center line and a driving under the influence (even though I blew a "0" in the Breathalyzer). In a sense, I was under the influence, but it wasn't alcohol or drugs. It was the insanity that had slowly taken control of me. I had left the house in such a hurry that I had forgotten to put on my pants. Thankfully I was wearing my boxers.

—·—

That November, three years after my son's death, I had to have my dog Chelsea euthanized. She had gotten old fast, probably from her own grief, and she was constantly stumbling and falling over. Mom said she was losing her dignity and it was time to release her from her pain-wracked body.

I applied that logic to myself. I was stumbling and falling, too.

I asked Valerie to drive me to the county police department so I could apologize if I did or said anything wrong, and while I was there I asked them to shoot me.

CHAPTER 23
INTERVENTION

THE POLICE considered it a suicide attempt. They arrested me and sent me to Frye Mental Institution for evaluation.

After five days, they released me to Northeast Psychological Center, an outpatient facility where I was diagnosed with depression and placed in group therapy.

Group sessions, to me, seemed pointless. I was bored. One day when I was leaving the group room, I noticed a woman from our group had fallen face down on the floor in the hall. I looked for help but there was no one around, so I turned her over onto her back and sat her up against the wall. Her head kept falling over, so I rubbed her face and squeezed her cheeks to revive her. She finally came to, and she said, "Thank you, Steve. I must have passed out. I think my blood sugar must have dropped."

The next thing I knew I was taken into a room and told by the staff that I had broken the rule against touching other patients. I tried to explain, but they wouldn't listen. They discharged me immediately.

I went back to the cemetery and told my son and God that I didn't understand what was happening. I did the best I could to help that woman, but I was punished for it.

—·—

A few months later, in April, 2006, I returned to Northeast Psychological Center, battling my relentless anger toward the ruination of my marriage and family. This time I was referred to psychologist John Norris, an ex-Marine Corp sergeant who seemed like a decent man. He asked about my faith, and asked personal questions, beyond the usual medical mumbo jumbo that I was used to hearing. He was a tough guy, like you'd expect a Marine sergeant to be, and that worked for me. Like a stern father, he was exactly the kind of doctor I needed.

He treated me like a fellow Marine. He put me through boot camp, and he vowed to take care of me.

Norris diagnosed me with post-traumatic stress syndrome, in addition to depression.

I began seeing him twice a week; on Tuesdays in a domestic violence group, and on Friday mornings for one-on-one therapy. I tried my best to talk to him as rationally as I could, but I almost got thrown out again when I screamed about not having insurance, when in fact I had two insurance policies that paid for everything.

That tough, old Marine showed great empathy, though at times he was pretty rough, chastising me about my self-pity and anger. After many months of treatment and education, I learned that doing the same thing over and over again and expecting different results was the definition of insanity. I was glad to know I wasn't crazy. I was insane.

After crying *every day* for three years and nine months, my psychologist, along with a prescription for Cymbalta, helped me stop.

One day he asked me, "You know what I think your wife might be?"

"Yeah, she's a whore."

"No, guess again."

"A whore who kills."

"You're getting close. I believe she might be a sociopath. Do you know what that is?"

"Someone that is mentally sick?"

"Yes, sick in a way that prevents her from having a conscience."

There was a medical diagnosis for what I'd been screaming about all this time. "Is that why she never cried over my boy?"

"Sociopaths don't cry. They don't experience feelings like other people do."

I told him how little Steve had oozed love, and how he told Angie every day, "I love you, Mommy!" as soon as he woke up, and all day long until he went to sleep every night.

"She couldn't feel love. This is a mental disorder, and it's expressed in many ways, one of which is an inability to feel sympathy or remorse." He went on to say that years ago, psychologists and psychiatrists would diagnose someone as a "sociopath" if the person exhibited certain behavior patterns, including: superficial charm, manipulation and cunning, a grandiose sense of self, a constant need for stimulation, lack of empathy, lack of remorse, or an inability to experience true love and shallow—if any—emotions. Sometimes, he told me, the individual's behavior might become so bizarre that others' lives are destroyed, and sometimes even death may occur.

Eventually, the term *sociopath* was replaced with *anti-social personality disorder*. But regardless of the title, the diagnostic criteria and attributes remain the same, as does the pain and the emotional scars inflicted on those who have tried to love and support someone with this disorder.

"If you really want to understand Angie," he said, "you have to stop judging her by normal standards."

He went to his bookcase and pulled out a big, fat book, opened it to a specific page and showed it to me.

"This is the *Diagnostic and Statistical Manual of Mental Disorders*, or *DSM* for short," he told me. "We use this to help us understand and diagnose our patients. I don't normally show this to patients, but I think it would be helpful for you to read this section."

He handed me the book and pointed to the section on antisocial personality disorder. I sat down and read it, slowly and carefully. And then I read it again, because it described Angie perfectly.

I had never felt so relieved about anything in my life. Here was an explanation for everything.

Ironically, this meant that I couldn't continue being so angry at her. It would be like being angry at a disabled person for not being able to walk. But Angie was not able to *love*. I couldn't blame her for that anymore than I could blame her for not being able to play a violin concerto. She just didn't know *how*.

I thought back to what I knew of her childhood... her mother Edith had chained her older brother up in a sweltering hot attic when he was a child. Her sister and her younger brother were both drug addicts, and the sister eventually murdered the brother to steal a few thousand bucks. Angie and her siblings had grown up in a sick environment.

I began to feel a little sorry for her.

But I also felt sorry for myself, and as much as I wanted to crawl in a hole and drown in my misery, it was time for me to wake up.

CHAPTER 24
OPENING UP

ON NOVEMBER 26, 2006, the fourth anniversary of my son's death, my mom and sister came to my house to celebrate Thanksgiving. While my sister cooked, my mom asked if she could have a look around.

"Sure, Mom, you don't have to ask." I headed toward my bedroom to lie down.

Soon my mom woke me. "Steven, get over here!"

I walked back into the dining room.

"What is this?" she asked, pointing to stacks of papers.

"My mail." There were four stacks, each about two feet high.

"What is going on here?"

"That's where I keep my mail."

"Don't you open it?"

"No."

"Why?"

"I don't know," I replied, and turned back toward my bedroom.

She raised her voice and said, "Oh no you don't! Get over here right now! What do you mean you don't open your mail?"

"I don't know."

"You don't know why? You're the only one that *does* know. Now why don't you open your mail?"

Embarrassed, I tried to explain, "Because I gave up. Because I don't need any more bad news. Because I'm afraid of everything and I don't want any correspondence from anyone. I don't have the money to pay my bills anymore anyway, so what's the point? I just want to be left alone."

And then she switched gears. "Don't worry about it, honey. It's Thanksgiving and it's almost time for dinner," she said. She walked into the kitchen and said, "I hope you like dessert."

"What is it?"

"Your mail."

We sat at the kitchen table, said our prayers, and ate our feast. While I was thankful for enjoying the meal with my mom and my sister, I dreaded dessert. So right after we ate I asked to be excused. I just wanted to go back to bed.

"No way, Steve. Bring your mail in here and let's open it."

When I got to the dining room table, I grabbed the first stack and felt sweat dripping off me. I carried it into the kitchen, grinding my teeth and said, "I have to go to bed."

"You can go to bed after we open your mail. Now go get the rest of it."

I got another stack, and was completely miserable. I didn't want to look at it, much less touch it.

I was utterly disgusted with myself. I had become afraid of my mail.

Midway through sorting through nine month's worth of mail, Mom looked up with a letter in her hand. "Steven, they're going to foreclose on your house."

I had stopped making payments months ago. In some part of my mind I knew this was bound to happen, but I hadn't let it bother me.

What did bother me was the tone of her voice as she tried to convey the seriousness of the situation. I could hear the words, but because I did not want to pay attention, I chose not to understand their meaning. This was what I had been doing with everyone around me for the past four years.

I didn't *want* to hear, so I *couldn't* hear. I felt the anger boiling up in side me, every muscle in my body tensed.

But then, she said, "It's okay. I'll help you."

Her calmness in that moment allowed me to loosen my grip on my tension, fear and anger. I sat down with Mom and actually *listened* to her for the first time in years.

"I know you're struggling with the memories, but I want you to know that they have consumed you to the point where you've given up on living, and I won't stand for that. I already lost a grandson, and I will not lose you, too. And speaking of little Steve, if you want to think about him all the time that's fine, but think about what HE would want. Would he want you to give up? Would he want you to be full of hate and fear? He'd want you to be the strong dad he remembers. He'd want to respect you, not worry about you or feel sorry for you."

I was speechless. *Why hadn't she said this to me before?*

Of course, she'd been saying this to me all along, over and over again, for years. I just hadn't wanted to hear it.

Now, facing my mail and my forthcoming foreclosure, it finally sunk in. What had changed? Was it because of my sessions with John Norris? Maybe it had something to do with finally understanding why Angie was the way she was. Maybe it was the medication I'd been prescribed. Or maybe it was all of the above. I don't know what it was, but I started to think about everything in a new way, as if I still had a son and I was still his father, and I had to be good father, not the man I'd been.

Instead of screaming, I just sat quietly.

Mom wrote a check to cover my unpaid taxes. As she handed it to me she said, "Go tomorrow and pay this. And from now on, OPEN your mail."

I told my psychologist about the mail and my revelation that I had still had to be a good father to Steve, and that I had to do this by being sane and functional.

And although I saw a faint light at the end of the tunnel, I still could not let go of my guilt. I had been asleep, under the influence of Xanax, when Angie killed my boy, and no matter what, I was responsible. I was responsible for trusting her to take care of him, and looking back, I see that I kept him and Jodi in a prison constructed and controlled by their psychotic mother. I had gone along with it. I had agreed to it. I had kept my family together for my own selfish needs. If I had left her, if I had paid attention to how sick and wrong everything was, Chub might still be alive. I was guilty. How could I ever get over that?

— · —

After several months of slowly waking up from the fog I'd been in for the past four years, I began to feel like an idiot about how I had lost my business. I asked my therapist if he thought I was strong enough to take Decorum and Darren Long to court for stealing half a million dollars from me.

"Yes, I think you are," he said. "But you'll need some help, because you aren't very good at explaining yourself clearly. I'll do my best to help you."

With my therapist's approval, and a newfound jolt of confidence, in February, 2007, I decided to see Merritt White, the lawyer who had originally represented me against Long.

After many phone calls and four visits to his office over a two-week period, Merritt White told me that there was nothing he could do. I then went to the lawyer who handled my divorce, and after reading through the paperwork, he said he couldn't help either, because he didn't want to clean up someone else's mess. Someone suggested I contact a high-profile lawyer in Charlotte, whose fee was $2,500 for the first four hours. When I balked at the price this attorney said, "I realize it's a lot of money, but it will show me how sincere you are."

Something about that answer—and the fact that he was so highly recommended— made me trust him. But of course I didn't have that kind of money, so I borrowed it from my mother. She was skeptical, but was happy to see me making an effort to repair my life. She wrote a check.

When I finally met with the attorney in Charlotte, he asked me first if I had received the letter he'd sent the previous week. I had to confess to my phobia about opening my mail which, of course, gave him the impression that I wasn't mentally stable. His letter had listed documents and materials that I was to bring to the meeting. I hadn't brought them. We didn't get off to a very good start.

He picked my case apart, I guess the way a high-priced lawyer should. He told me that I'd had good counsel, but that the statute of limitations had expired. He also asked me what I'd been doing the past four years and why I hadn't pursued the matter sooner.

And I dug an even deeper hole for myself by explaining that I'd spent the last four years crying over my son, trying to figure out why my wife was a sociopath, recovering from the accident and losing my ability to think clearly and function normally. I broke down in tears and told him everything about my guilt, my paranoia, the mental hospitals—all of it.

I knew I was going about this all wrong, and of course I wasn't surprised that he didn't take my case. I left his office in tears.

I cried all the way home, humiliated and defeated, not only by the intimidating lawyer, but by the embarrassment of wasting my mother's money.

CHAPTER 25
ALIVE!

GUILT NOW WEIGHED more heavily than ever before. Just when I thought I moving toward recovery, my one step forward ended up being two steps back.

My guilt turned to self-hatred and I spent my time lying in bed or going to the cemetery and begging God to bring my son back.

Close to the fifth anniversary of Steve's death, I went to the cemetery to put flowers on his grave. Valerie joined me there While I was pulling weeds, she handed me a little white angel. "Here's an angel for your little angel."

I placed it on his grave, and a giant wave of anger toward Angie hit me again.

"It's going on five years now and she hasn't even put a flower on his grave, I'm embarrassed for her. What a disgrace."

"Steve, this is a holy place. Don't bring her here with you. Be proud of what you are, and honor your son with your presence and everything that is good in you. Don't pollute yourself and your son's memory with any more thoughts of her. It's time for you to move on now. Let's celebrate Steve's life instead of dwelling on the darkness."

She was right of course.

When I got home I went straight to bed, but was woken by the phone. The caller ID said "unknown number," and the caller hung up as soon as I answered. For some reason, this made me laugh out loud. It had been more than two years since I'd had a call from an unknown number, and that call had been from Angie. I knew it was her calling, and I laughed about how perfectly appropriate it was for her to be identified as an unknown person.

It had been years since I'd laughed.

I went back to the cemetery that night. "Okay, God," I said. "All right, you win. He's yours; I give up. I thank you for letting me have him for the brief time he was here on earth. Please take care of him."

I woke up the next day and felt odd. I was calm. I felt different. I felt alive. Even my face felt different. Wait a minute... I was *smiling!*

I walked into my son's room and instead of heart-wrenching sadness, I felt joy when I looked at his picture above the bed. I lay down on his bed and thought about all the wonderful times I had shared with him and how truly blessed I was to have had him in my life.

I felt alive! I was so excited that I had to tell Mom, my sister, and Valerie. I was alive!

"I don't know, Mom. I just feel different. I'm not as sad as I was. Yesterday I guess I just finally gave up. I gave in to God, and realized that I can't change what happened. All this time I was thinking that if I was angry and guilty enough, somehow it would change things. But when I got up this morning, something was different. Maybe I slowed down just enough to see that I can't change anything. All I can do is bear witness to what I have seen and what I know, so I gave back to God what he blessed me with, and he gave me back my soul."

Mom hugged me and said, "Well, it's about time."

—·—

My therapist asked if my mother would make a list comparing what I was like now versus what I was like before I met Angie, she said that would be easy. "Before Angie," she said, "you were full of life. My house was full of life whenever you were here. Now you're just a room full of pain. You lost the sparkle in your eyes. But don't worry about the sparkle, be thankful for the sight. The sparkle will come back with the thanks you give over time."

What a wise, amazing woman she was. I could never have survived this without her. I was suddenly filled with gratitude, not just for my mom, but for my son, and for John Norris, and Valerie, and all the good things in my world. I was still angry at Angie of course, but I had a feeling I could express that anger differently now. Over the years I'd written her dozens of angry letters (I sent none of them), and they were full of rage. I wondered if it would be different to write her a letter now. So I sat down and gave it a try, vowing to write it from my son and me, together.

NOW THAT I AM GONE

Now that I am gone,
Do you ever think of what once was?
To be so alive with life,
Which is what the gift of love just does.
My unfortunate encounter
With you so great,
Now with only words,
I will try to recreate.
The promises you made,
That really weren't there,
Are the empty dreams,
That I must now bear.
The lies you fed,
As food for encouragement,
Were really poison,
That were desired for nourishment.
Your tainted love,
Was fed with your every breath,
You are the poison,
That spreads the plague of death.

And while you continue,
Your wrath as you go on,
I live once again,
Now that I am gone.

About a month later I walked to the mailbox (I was now reading my mail on a more or less regular basis), and on top of the stack was an envelope with only the word: *Steve*. My first thought, of course, was fear. *Now what?*

I opened the envelope and pulled out a picture of a very pretty young lady in a white graduation robe holding a rose, smiling. I didn't know who it was, but she did have a familiar look about her. I flipped the picture over and was floored to discover that it was Jodi! My little Jodi graduated from high school... and she'd remembered me! An overwhelming sense of pride and happiness flooded through me, and as I flipped the photo back over to gaze at my beautiful little girl. I noticed there was a letter in the envelope, half written to me, and other half written to my mom:

Dad (Steve),

You were always and will be the father I never had. My father Frank, as you already know, knows nothing about me and never will. But you and I were close. I loved you and saw you as my father. Now I just want you to know I have never forgotten you and I will always love you. I'm very sorry for what happened and that we haven't kept in touch. If Chelsea is still alive give her my love too!

Grandma,

I love you so very much. I hope you are not mad at me for not keeping in touch. You are an amazing person and a

> *great grandmother! You are a great chef, you have a warm heart, and are so very kind. I hope you can find it in your heart to forgive me. I miss you soooooooooooo much Grandma, I hope you still love me too, because I really love you! You are special to me still! I am growing up and wish you could see me now!*

I was so proud to be called Dad again! That little three letter word allowed me to enter into the garden of family sanctity; a place where there is true love and innocence. Jodi's respect and love pulled me back into that beautiful world and left me with a sense of hope. I was overwhelmed with joy, and this time, I cried happy tears instead of tears of misery. Jodi brought back the greatest love of my life... love of my children.

I wrote Jodi a letter in return:

> *Congratulations on your graduation! I am so very proud of you. I must try to explain, I had no choice about loving you. You stole my heart when I first saw you. You were something so special. When you were a baby, every time I looked down at you, I was really looking up to you. The inquisitiveness of your youth kept me sharp, the youthful exuberance of your childhood kept me young, and your kindness made life beautiful. That is why I must thank you for being so kind for allowing me to look up to you with the admiration that you so commanded with these God given traits.*
>
> *Jodi, yes we were close, and boy did I, and still do, love you! The only way I can best describe the love I have for you is when I used to call you 'My little girl' and you would call me 'Dad'. The trust that we put in those words is what made it all so special. YOU ARE STILL MY LITTLE GIRL!*
>
> *I have not for one moment stopped thinking about you and your*

brother. Your brother was a wonderful boy, and I want you to know that I loved you both the same. You both weren't 'he' or 'she,' you were the most special things in my heart, soul and life. You were my children.

You made it so easy being Dad because of the innocence of the love you gave. It was magic! It was because of this that I must thank you.

Chelsea is gone. She passed on about three months after you left. Grandma and Joanne love and miss you also

They say when you love something and let it go, if it comes back, it is because of the love that was instilled into it, and so it was meant to be. I thank you for coming back. You were a wonderful little girl, and I can tell by the eloquence of your writing, that you are now a wonderful young lady.

Please Jodi, do not be sorry, for you have done nothing wrong. Be proud of what you are, and be the best you can be. Thank you for the blessing of joy that you have given me. You have now helped me more than you can ever imagine.

Sincerely loving you always,

DAD

During the weeks that followed Jodi's letter, everyday life seemed to be a little more tolerable. I was calmer, and could handle life's little imperfections better. At one point Angie called. I listened to her politely for a minute or two, then got off the phone quickly, without arguing, accusing, or trying to figure out why she did the things she did. It was incredibly freeing for me. I realized that I didn't have to waste my time thinking about her, and with my doctor's help, I was learning that it's impossible to make sense of sociopathic behavior. All this time I thought I had to figure it out; to retrace her steps and replay every scene in my mind a thousand times, looking for clues. But I never found any clues. Instead, I discovered that Angie likely was a sociopath, and although it was beyond my control to repair any of the damage she'd done, this was enough to give me a measure of peace.

EPILOGUE

TODAY, I AM embarrassed to admit how naive I was, and how willing I had been to turn a blind eye to my wife's lies, manipulations and most importantly, as I learned later, her mental illness.

I didn't know how to respond to her bizarre and dangerous behaviors. I did not address her neglect of the children, was blind to her affairs with other men, confused, and then angered by her lack of concern or remorse.

Ironically, my desire to keep my family together ultimately broke us apart; even while I believed I was doing my best to protect them, I had put them at risk.

From the first, I was fooled by Angie's behavior and didn't recognize how she manipulated me. Eventually, she molded me into exactly what she accused me of being: suspicious and controlling. And now, recalling the horrible things I said to her in the heat of anger, I realize that I had sunk to her level.

I was deceived from the very beginning. For instance, the paper she showed me soon after we first met—the paper she claimed was a restraining order against her then-husband Frank—proved to be nothing more than a parking ticket.

Looking back, that was probably the moment I fell head-first into her web, and, paralyzed like a fly, I was unable to escape. She made me disregard my instincts and turn my back on rational thinking.

Worse than the non-existent restraining order was the blatant untruth regarding her older daughter Mary's custody. Years after our divorce, I learned that Angie decided on a whim one day, before we moved to North Carolina, to relinquish Mary to her ex-husband. However, she hadn't informed Frank of her decision and he wasn't home when she arrived at his house that winter day. Regardless, Angie left nine-year-old Mary on Frank's snow-covered doorstep. Mary sat there for hours until her father came home from work.

My therapist suggests that Mary had reached an age where she was too old and too smart to be fooled by her mother's games and lies. At that age, girls often speak out and question their parents, and Angie was afraid that Mary's growing awareness would disrupt the false life she was trying to create with me. She later repeated this behavior with Jodi.

Many years later, when Mary was in her late twenties, she found me through Google. We talked for a long time. She got pregnant at age 16, and Frank threw her out, forcing her to live on the streets. Over the next dozen years, Mary had five children, four of whom were taken away by social services. When she called me, she asked a question that shattered my heart, "Why did you and Mom throw me away?"

I tried to explain that I wasn't part of that plan. She asked why I didn't try to save her, and I did not have a good answer. All I can say to justify my actions—or lack of actions—was that I was under Angie's spell and had lost my ability to think clearly.

As for her extra source of money, when we barely had two pennies to rub together? It turns out that Angie told my mother a hard luck story about not having enough money to make ends meet, and convinced my mother to write checks for several of our household bills each month. But at the same time, I was giving her cash from my paycheck to pay those very bills. Angie kept the cash while mom paid for our electricity, cable, and other utilities, to the tune of about $800 a month.

— · —

As the years went by, friends, neighbors and co-workers came forward with more information that helped unravel the web of lies that had entrapped me.

Angie's workplace had been important to her not because of her paycheck, but because of the extracurricular activities that kept her busy seven days a week. I bought into her "I have a lot of work to do" story for years, until I found out about the long list of boyfriends she had at work. She had sex in the store room, the parking lot, bathroom stalls, and anywhere else where she could a get fix of drama, control, validation and what the psychiatric community calls "narcissistic supply." Sweet old Wilma, back when Angie and I first met, had tried to warn me.

I learned that Angie had influence in the stores where I worked because she was having sex with so many of the employees and some of the managers as well. She had convinced them all that I beat her and abused the kids.

Her stories spread and most of the town believed them. Not knowing these stories were circulating, I never tried to defend myself.

Angie had not limited her affairs to men who worked in convenience and grocery stores. She also had an affair with a Concord police officer. I can't say for certain if that's why the Concord police ignored my theft reports when I owned the vending machine franchise, but it was the beginning of a series of frustrating encounters with the authorities where Angie was involved.

More than a decade later, while shopping at a local grocery store, a woman I had only recently met asked me my ex-wife's name. When I told her, she said, "I knew it! I thought that was her. Your wife was a dancer at Baby Dolls and she had a cop for a boyfriend. In fact, he was her pimp."

"What?" I was stunned.

"Yeah," she said, "She was a real celebrity in this town until you threw her out and she ended up in the battered women's shelter. I heard you had been beating her and your kids for years."

Angie had done to me what she'd done to her first husband, Frank.

Her lies, her manipulations, and all the judgments imposed on me as a result—it was almost too much to comprehend.

—·—

Eight and a half years after my son's death, mom said that Angie told her that I had given her Xanax the day of the accident. It turns out that Angie had arranged to meet her police officer boyfriend in Baltimore for the Thanksgiving weekend. She planned to take little Steve with her, drop Jodi at a friend's house, and leave me home alone. In our kitchen, before setting off on this adventure, Angie took both of the blue Xanax tablets she'd taken from me (four times the amount she would most likely have been prescribed) and washed them down with a rum and Coke. A stiff rum and Coke, more rum than Coke at a ratio of six to one.

It is important to note that Xanax and alcohol are a deadly combination; both are central nervous system depressants, slowing how the body sends, receives, and processes information. The combination of these two chemicals causes intense confusion, decreased reaction time, and an almost complete lack of motor skills. In addition, both substances work on the same neurotransmitters and receptors in the brain; combining Xanax and alcohol increases each chemical's effect.

When Angie left our house she was both drunk and under the influence of prescription drugs. Her motor skills and decision-making abilities seriously compromised. So it was not surprising that she hadn't buckled our son in his car seat. She had the stereo blasting and windows down when she lost control of her car. Steve flew out the open window. The car flipped and landed on him. A witness said Angie crawled out of the car, over Steve, and ran into the road screaming for help. He was alive for about twenty minutes after impact.

—·—

For me, the awareness of my wife's true nature came far too late, at a cost that can never be repaid. It is my hope that by writing this book and sharing my story, I might be able to alert someone, somewhere, to the warning signs, in time to save marriages, minds, families, and *lives*.

I now putter around my house and survive on monthly disability checks. I'm thankful for my physical health, and I'm thankful for the beautiful memories of my son Steve and the knowledge that I am still his dad, because death cannot truly separate us. When I think of him without anger, I feel his presence, and instead of sadness, I am filled with happiness.

Regarding Angie, therapy has allowed me to see that she is sick, just like someone with cancer or a severe disability. I still want to scream when I think of the pain she caused, but I now know that she is in just as much pain, and has been her entire life; she just deals with it in a very different way.

I've let go of the fury that once controlled my life. I want to be free of it.

ACKNOWLEDGEMENTS

I am eternally grateful to John Norris, who, through his experience, gave me knowledge, wisdom, and showed me that there is a different way to understand my losses.

I am grateful to my beloved mother, whose love, patience, and prayers kept me alive. My mother passed as was I finishing this book, and because she was very ill and suffering, it was a relief to see her go. She knew she was going to see her grandson and my father, and she was at peace with that. The last words she spoke to me were, "I am going to be with your father and take care of your boy..." Through her, I learned to see death in a new way, and as a result, I now see that God doesn't necessarily work the way we think He should. We don't need to beg and fight, because life goes on no matter what, and it's more important to see the purpose behind our bad experiences than to scream and cry and beg for them to disappear.

The DA's office in Cabarrus County created a wall of photos of children who have died, and my son Steve's photo was the first one to be hung there. My son's death launched a tradition of memorializing these beautiful children, and now they can be remembered by anyone who walks into that office. I am honored and grateful that my son and others are being remembered in this way.

I was granted new life after a terrible mental and spiritual death. I am now a thankful, humbled man.

CPSIA information can be obtained
at www.ICGtesting.com
Printed in the USA
FFOW04n0110160916
27627FF

9 781684 197316